MIS... LITTLE BOOK OF ANSWERS

MISSIONARY'S
LITTLE BOOK OF ANSWERS

GILBERT SCHARFFS

Covenant Communications, Inc.
Covenant

Cover image *Christ at Emmaus* by Walter Rane © Intellectual Reserve, Inc.
Courtesy of Museum of Church History and Art.

Cover design copyrighted 2002 by Covenant Communications, Inc.

Published by Covenant Communications, Inc.
American Fork, Utah

Printed in the United States of America
First Printing: June 2002

09 08 07   10 9 8 7

ISBN 1-59156-038-1

Library of Congress Cataloging-in-Publication Data

TABLE OF CONTENTS

CHAPTER EIGHT: *Allegations Clarified*

INTRODUCTION

*"Sanctify the Lord God in your hearts:
and be ready to give an answer to
every man that asketh"*
(1 PETER 3:15)

In 1985, the Communications Department of
The Church of Jesus Christ of Latter-day Saints asked
me to respond to an anti-LDS book and movie called
The Godmakers. My reply was published in 1986, followed by a second edition in 1989, both titled *The
Truth About the Godmakers.* Since then, I have
received hundreds of letters and phone calls asking
for answers to additional questions. As a teacher at
the LDS Institute of Religion, I found myself counseling people troubled by anti-Mormon material.
Many of them had been referred to me by other
teachers, bishops, stake and mission presidents. After
my book was published, I also received requests to
speak to LDS and non-LDS groups concerning criticisms of the LDS Church.

It was suggested by some colleagues and church leaders that I write a general response book. This book attempts to give answers to the most commonly asked questions about the LDS Church. Most material critical of the Church raises the same charges that have been made since the earliest days of the LDS Church. I began preliminary work in 1987, but let family, teaching classes, attending to church callings and other writing projects take precedence.

I again sensed the need to hasten work on this manuscript when asked by the editors of the *Ensign* to respond to a letter they had received. What follows is the question and my reply that appeared in the January 1995 *Ensign,* 61–62:

> *Some people say it is best to leave materials alone that claim to "expose" the Church and its teachings. What counsel is there on this? How do we respond when a friend comes to us with questions found in such materials?*

When President Brigham Young was asked why the Church did not publish the truth regarding lies circulated about the Latter-day Saints, he replied: "We might do this if we owned all the papers published in Christendom" (*Discourses of Brigham Young,* ed. John A. Widtsoe, [1978], 352).

Today, as in President Young's day, General Authorities usually do not comment on negative information about the Church. Their responsibility is to proclaim the gospel of Jesus Christ. Their primary work is to "bear testimony of the restoration of the gospel and that Jesus is the Christ" (*Church News*, 18 Dec. 1983, 2). They know, as the Lord revealed to Isaiah, that "no weapon formed against thee shall prosper" (Isa. 54:17).

However, when the occasion requires a response, Church leaders do answer specific critics and criticisms to set the record straight. Latter-day doctrines and practices are not on trial. Gospel principles are God-given eternal truths that bless faithful members and the world at large.

Elder Bruce R. McConkie of the Quorum of the Twelve likened the Church to a great organized caravan following an appointed course. "What does it matter if a few barking dogs snap at the heels of the weary travelers? . . . The caravan moves on" (*Ensign*, Nov. 1984, 85).

The restored gospel centers on teachings that save, strengthen, uplift, inspire, and bind individuals and families. The Church discourages teachings contrary to such goals. Because of their great concern for the membership, Church leaders have given guidance concerning anti-LDS material. They caution against those things designed to destroy belief and cause pain and suffering.

President Ezra Taft Benson has advised against purchasing material derogatory to the

Church, explaining that buying this material will only "help sustain their cause" (Address to religious educators, 17 Sept. 1976). And Elder Carlos E. Asay of the Seventy has warned against those who attempt to "sow doubts and disturb the peace of true believers. . . . Avoid those who would tear down your faith. Faith-killers are to be shunned. The seeds which they plant in the minds and hearts of men grow like cancer and eat away the Spirit" (*Ensign*, Nov. 1981, 67–68).

Such advice does not mean that the Church is against honest scholarship or has anything to fear or hide. Nor does the Church ban literature, but Latter-day Saints should be wise in choosing what to read. This cautionary counsel should not justify laziness on our part in seeking answers or giving glib, superficial replies. When someone sincerely wants to know the truth after reading anti-LDS material, we should find an answer. We must not allow Church critics and enemies to make, what Elder Neal A. Maxwell of the Quorum of Twelve has called, "uncontested slam dunks."

The Church encourages gospel scholarship and the search for truth. "Fundamental to our theology is belief in individual freedom and inquiry, thought, and expression. Constructive discussion is a privilege of every Latter-day Saint," said President Gordon B. Hinckley of the First Presidency (*Ensign*, Sept. 1985, 6).

Latter-day Saints should be sufficiently grounded in their testimonies and knowledge of Church doctrine and history so that they can answer questions in a noncontentious and informative way. Elder Marvin J. Ashton of the Quorum of the Twelve has instructed Church members not to retaliate against attacks. "We encourage all our members to refuse to become anti-anti-Mormon," he said (*Ensign*, Nov. 1991, 63). The Apostle Paul taught that coming to Christ requires "speaking the truth in love" (Eph. 4:15).

The First Presidency has encouraged Church members to convey their response to questions "with positive explanations of doctrines and practices of the Church" (*Church News*, 18 Dec. 1983, 2). Members should invite those with questions about Church doctrine and practices to read latter-day scriptures and to study the restored gospel, thus tasting the gospel fruit for themselves. Only then will they know "whether it be of God" (John 7:17).

When members lack answers, they should learn what leaders and reputable scholars have said and written. There is probably no charge against the Church not adequately refuted by someone. When members cannot find answers on their own, they can turn to home and visiting teachers, quorum leaders, bishops and stake presidents. If necessary, stake presidents can take questions to area presidencies or other authorities.

During a Church fireside, Elder Boyd K. Packer of the Quorum of the Twelve referred to the Jews' undeviating course in rebuilding the wall around Jerusalem, following their return from captivity (*Ensign*, Aug. 1983, 68–71). The prophet Nehemiah, who directed the work, would not be lured away by his enemies, telling them, "I am doing a great work, . . . why should the work cease, whilst I leave it, and come down to you?" (Neh. 6:3).

In relating how Latter-day Saints should react to public ridicule of sacred temple and priesthood ordinances, Elder Packer said, "That is what we should do: Go about our work, strengthening the wards and the stakes, the quorums and the families and the individual members. We have a work to do. Why should it cease while we do battle with our enemies? . . . Do not be drawn away to respond to enemies" (*Ensign*, Aug. 1983, 69).

The Church of Jesus Christ of Latter-day Saints is true and will continue to bring peace of mind and purpose of life to many. Those who would reap great eternal rewards and joy must wisely use their time to study, ponder, pray, and live the gospel so they can anchor their convictions in the Lord and Savior Jesus Christ and His Church.

* * * * * * * * *

Since few people have access to the many written responses available to questions about the Church, this handbook will hopefully be helpful. Most answers are intentionally brief, unless a longer answer is appropriate. However, for most questions, there are suggestions for further reading.

It is my experience that confronting avowed enemies of the Church is unproductive and usually leads to unpleasant and angry confrontations; "He that has the spirit of contention is not of me, but is of the devil, who is the father of contention and he stirreth up the hearts of men to contend with anger, one against another" (3 Ne. 11:29). Answering critics will seldom change their minds. However, sincere friends, family members, investigators and the public deserve answers. The preacher in Ecclesiastes said, "There is a time to keep silence, and a time to speak" (Eccl. 3:7). The purpose of this book is to make honest responses readily available and to encourage further gospel study. "Whoso treasureth up my word, shall not be deceived" (J.S. Matt. 1:37).

EXPLANATION: The Church of Jesus Christ of Latter-day Saints is the official name of the church that is sometimes called the Mormon Church and its members Mormons. However, using the full title, The Church of Jesus Christ of Latter-day Saints, several times in each paragraph would be awkward, redundant and space consuming. Therefore, when appropriate, other commonly used names are substituted: Latter-day Saints, LDS Church, LDS members, Mormons and the Church.

BIBLE QUOTES: The King James Version is cited unless otherwise indicated.

DISCLAIMER: The interpretations of Latter-day Saint doctrine in this book reflect the understanding of the author and are not necessarily the official views of The Church of Jesus Christ of Latter-day Saints.

NOTES: Scriptural references are included in the main body of the text. Citations of books and articles are referred to in the text by author, year of publication, and page number. A more detailed reference is given in the bibliography at the end of the book.

ABBREVIATIONS: Standard abbreviations of biblical books that have lengthy names are used.
For *History of the Church, HC* is used.
For *Journal of Discourses, JD* is used.
For *Foundation for Ancient Research and Mormon Studies, F.A.R.M.S.* is used.
For *Encyclopedia of Mormonism, EM* is used.

CHAPTER ONE
Commonly Asked Questions

1.1. Isn't the LDS Church different from other Christian churches?

To fault one religion for being different is to fault every religion. All religions in the world differ from each other. This is especially true of Christianity, which has far more subdivisions than any other world religion. Every Christian church, including the LDS Church, has similarities with Judaism, Buddhism, Hinduism, Shintoism, Confucianism, Islam and other world religions. However, Mormonism has the most in common with the rest of Christianity, since Christ is uppermost to Christians, including Latter-day Saints. See Appendix A: "A Few Brief Similarities and Differences Between Today's 'Mainstream Christianity' and The Church of Jesus Christ of Latter-day Saints."

Further Reading: Hickenbotham.

1.2. Are Latter-day Saints Christians?

The title—The Church of Jesus Christ of Latter-day Saints—should make it clear that Latter-day Saints are Christians. The Savior's followers used His name to represent themselves in biblical times. Paul wrote: "The churches of Christ salute you," indicating that early Christian churches in New Testament times used the name of Christ in referring to their organization as do Latter-day Saints today (Rom. 16:16). Besides using the name of Jesus Christ in its title, the Church also accepts many of the same biblical doctrines as other Christian churches. However, the LDS Church also believes in numerous biblical concepts changed or forgotten by many Christian denominations, which could arguably make the LDS Church more Christian than other Christians.

According to most dictionaries, a Christian is one "professing belief in Jesus Christ and following His teachings as recorded in the Bible." This qualifies Latter-day Saints, who not only believe in Christ, but unequivocally testify of the divinity of the Savior. The keystone of the LDS Church is exactly as the title of its book of scripture suggests—The Book of Mormon: Another Testament of Jesus Christ. This additional witness of our Lord and Savior mentions Him every two verses on average. It contains an account of His ministry to the Western Hemisphere following His crucifixion and resurrection in

Jerusalem. One verse says, "We talk of Christ, we rejoice in Christ, we preach of Christ and we prophesy of Christ" (2 Ne. 25:26).

1.3. Why is calling the LDS Church non-Christian illogical?

Some justify calling the LDS Church non-Christian because it has some doctrinal differences with other Christian churches. This does not seem like a logical reason since there is much disagreement among all Christian churches over doctrine. There are often major differences between conservative and liberal wings of the same church. For example, former President Jimmy Carter, probably the most visible member of his church, recognizes the inappropriateness of fellow Christians who wish to deny those not of their faith the title of Christian. He disagrees with leaders in his church and has said that Mormons are Christians. "I think that among the worst things we can do as believers in Christ, is to condemn others who confess faith in Christ and try to have a narrow definition of who is and who is not an acceptable believer and a child of God" (*Deseret News*, April 3, 1998, sec. A, p. 1). President Carter also disagrees with his church on numerous other issues, but has never been called a non-Christian by his church's leaders (*Salt Lake Tribune,* November 22, 1997, sec. C., p. 1).

Whether you are Hinayana, Mahayana or any of the subgroups, you are still considered a Buddhist. If you are Sunni, Shiite, Suffi, you are called a Muslim. Whether Orthodox, Conservative, Reform, Liberal, Reconstructionist, or Hasidic, you are Jewish. If you are Catholic, Orthodox, Protestant, or any of the subgroups, you are Christian. Thus, it is illogical to say that if you are a member of The Church of Jesus Christ of Latter-day Saints, you are not a Christian.

Further Readings: Hickenbotham (1995), 89; Winward (1995), 55.

1.4. Do Latter-day Saints believe all other churches are false?

This is a perception some have of Mormonism, but it is far from how the LDS Church views others. Actually, Latter-day Saint doctrine maintains there is truth to be found in other religions and institutions. The Church's thirteenth article of faith states in part: "If there is anything virtuous, lovely, or of good report or praiseworthy, we seek after these things." In the Book of Mormon we read, "The Lord doth grant unto all nations . . . all that he seeth fit that they should have" (Alma 29:8). In the same volume of scripture the Lord says: "All men are privileged the one like unto the other, and none are forbidden" (2 Ne. 26:28). "We see that God is mindful of every people whatsoever land they may be in; yea he numbereth his people, and his bowels of mercy are over all the earth" (Alma 26:37). Therefore, the Lord has blessed His children with portions of light and knowledge through most religions.

Joseph Smith taught, "The Lord deals with his people as a tender parent with a child, communicating light and intelligence and the knowledge of his ways as they can bear it" (*HC*, V, 402). The LDS Church made the following official statement regarding God's love for all mankind:

* * * * * * * * * *

STATEMENT OF THE FIRST PRESIDENCY REGARDING GOD'S LOVE FOR ALL MANKIND

"Based upon ancient and modern revelation, The Church of Jesus Christ of Latter-day Saints gladly teaches and declares the Christian doctrine that all men and women are brothers and sisters, not only by blood relationship from common mortal progenitors, but also as literal spirit children of an Eternal Father.

"The great religious leaders of the world such as Mohammed, Confucius, and the Reformers, as well as philosophers including Socrates, Plato, and others, received a portion of God's light. Moral truths were given to them by God to enlighten whole nations and to bring a higher level of understanding to individuals.

"The Hebrew prophets prepared the way for the coming of Jesus Christ, the promised Messiah, who should provide salvation for all mankind who believe in the gospel. Consistent with these truths, we believe that God has given and will give to all peoples sufficient knowledge to help them on their way to eternal salvation, either in this life or in the life to come.

"We also declare that the gospel of Jesus Christ, restored to His Church in our day, provides the only way to a mortal life of happiness and a fulness of joy forever. For those who have not received this gospel, the opportunity will come to them in the life hereafter if not in this life.

"Our message, therefore, is one of special love and concern for the eternal welfare of all men and women, regardless of religious belief, race or nationality, knowing that we are brothers and sisters because we are sons and daughters of the same Eternal Father" (Palmer, 1978, frontpiece).

The attitude of the LDS Church toward others is evidenced by their involvement with other religions. An example of this spirit of cooperation was shown at a special meeting in Washington, D.C. in 1998. With diplomats from sixteen Islamic nations watching, the Church and BYU introduced the first in a series of translations of centuries-old classical

writings of great Muslim scholars. LDS officials present were Elder Neal A. Maxwell of the Council of the
Twelve and BYU president Merrill J. Bateman. The
Deseret News reported that these "LDS officials said
they are leading such efforts both to build friendships
with Muslims and because of LDS doctrine that truth
should be sought wherever it may be, even if that is
in centuries-old Islamic writings never before available in English" (*Deseret News,* 7 February 1998, sec.
E., p. 1).

Another area of religious cooperation to seek
religious truths is an ongoing project of the
Foundation for Ancient Research and Mormon
Studies (F.A.R.M.S.) sponsored by the LDS Church.
This organization preserves fragile ancient religious
artifacts in electronic formats. Also conserved in this
manner are the texts of the complete Dead Sea Scrolls
and data from the F.A.R.M.S. Syriac, Bonampak, and
Petra projects. In addition F.A.R.M.S. has compiled
Islamic Hadith and Tibetan Buddhist scriptural texts
called sutras. All this invaluable data is available to
religious scholars around the world for research
(*Insights,* May 1999, 3).

1.5. Does the LDS Church claim to be the only true church?

Most churches believe they are the true, or at
least the best church. That is one reason why there are

so many different churches. Latter-day Saints do claim that the fulness of the gospel of Jesus Christ was restored through the prophet Joseph Smith. However, Mormonism recognizes there are truths and good people in other churches, as the official statement by the Church in the previous answer declared. Latter-day Saints do not believe they have a monopoly on truth. LDS scripture teaches "religion is instituted of God" (D&C 134:4).

In a free pluralistic society such as the United States we have the right to disagree, but not to persecute or belittle. Religious liberty is an underlying principle that has made and kept our nation free and strong. Therefore, it is most inappropriate when anyone strives to persecute and tear down others who do not believe as they do. The LDS Church's eleventh article of faith is a remarkable statement dealing with the ideal relationship between differing religions: "We claim the privilege of worshiping Almighty God according to the dictates of our own conscience, and allow all men the same privilege. . . ." On one occasion, John said to Jesus: "We saw one casting out devils in thy name; and we forbad him, because he followeth not with us." Our attitude toward others should be that of the Savior, who said to His disciples, "Forbid him not; for he that is not against us is for us" (Luke 9:49–50).

Further Readings: EM (1992) 1:45–52, 3:1076; Griffith (1989), 103.

1.6. Do Latter-day Saints want to convert everyone to their church?

Latter-day Saints do not expect to convert everyone to their church. However, they know from over one hundred and seventy-two years of experience that there are many people on Earth waiting to hear the message of the restored gospel. Latter-day Saints seek those willing to listen. Whether such individuals join the LDS Church is their choice. Since members of the Church believe they have the fulness of the gospel of Jesus Christ, a perfect plan of joy and happiness, they have the responsibility to offer it to everyone.

Latter-day Saints do not believe that Christ would want His Church to be a private club. This was made clear when the Lord charged His followers: "Go ye therefore, and teach all nations, baptizing them in the name of the Father, and of the Son, and of the Holy Ghost" (Matt. 28:19). When Church members see positive changes in converts who have found new purpose and understanding of life, all the efforts are worthwhile.

Many Christian and non-Christian churches have missionary programs. Latter-day Saints feel compelled to retain the original mandate from the Lord and their commitment to share their beliefs (Mark 15:15).

1.7. Why does the LDS Church refer to its members as "Saints"?

The name of the Church came through a revelation from the Lord (See D&C 115). Because the word "saint" in modern usage has evolved to designate deceased individuals who were heroic Christians during their lifetime, it does seem arrogant. However, using "saint" to define a noble person who has died is not found anywhere in scripture. Since the word "Saint(s)" appears nearly one hundred times in the Bible to identify *living* followers of Christ, this seems to be the reason the Lord wanted His disciples in the latter days to adhere to this biblical practice.

Latter-day Saints have human weaknesses and shortcomings. To Church members, the title "Saints" is a goal to strive for by living high ideals and following Christ's admonition: "If ye love me, keep my commandments" (John 14:15).

Further Readings: Griffith (1959), 25; *EM* (1992) 2:806, 3:1249; Peterson and Ricks (1992), 1–191; Winwood (1995), 30–32.

1.8. Do Latter-day Saints believe in a different Jesus from most Christians?

Latter-day Saints agree with many Christians that Jesus was the son of Virgin Mary, is divine, suffered and died on the cross for our sins, and was resurrected, overcoming His own death and ours. Latter-day

Saints also agree with some other Christians (a small minority) who maintain that Christ is the literal, separate Son of God, who has a resurrected body today, and is a separate being in the Godhead. Latter-day Saints completely disagree with those Christians who say that Jesus was only mortal (in no way divine) or that the accounts of Him are allegorical.

President Gordon B. Hinckley has acknowledged that critics may assert we do not believe in the traditional Christ of Christianity.

> Our faith, our knowledge is not based on ancient tradition, the creeds which came of a finite understanding and out of the almost infinite discussions of men trying to arrive at a definition of the risen Christ. Our faith, our knowledge comes of the witness of a prophet in this dispensation who saw before him the great God of the universe and His Beloved Son, the resurrected Lord Jesus Christ. They spoke to him. He spoke with them. He testified openly, unequivocally, and unabashedly of that great vision. It was a vision of the Almighty and of the Redeemer of the world, glorious beyond our understanding but certain and unequivocating in the knowledge which it brought (in Conference Report, Apr. 2002).

19

Further Readings: Hickenbotham (1995), 14–15; Peterson (1995), 71–74; Peterson and Ricks (1992), 25–27.

1.9. Since Mormons do not accept the Trinity, does this disqualify them as Christians?

The Bible never mentions the word "Trinity," nor do most dictionaries in defining Christians. Non-LDS Christians disagree among themselves on the meaning of the Trinity, and many admit they do not comprehend it. Some Christians say Trinity means "One God manifests himself in three different forms: Father, Son and Holy Ghost." Others, as do several dictionaries, say that "Trinity is the *union* of three divine figures: Father, Son and Holy Ghost." Latter-day Saints agree with this latter definition, believing that the Godhead signifies a *union of purpose*, as the Bible teaches, and *not a union of body*, as some Trinitarians believe. Latter-day Saints agree with those non-LDS Christians who believe that the Godhead consists of three separate personages.

The Bible clearly teaches a Godhead of separate beings. At His baptism, Jesus stood in the water, and God the Father, speaking from heaven, stated, "This is my beloved Son, in whom I am well pleased" (Matt. 3:17). God used the same words in introducing His Son on the Mount of Transfiguration (See Matt. 17:5).

Also, when Christ was agonizing on the cross, He cried, "O my Father; not as I will, but as thou wilt"

(See Matt. 26:39–42). In a vision, Stephen saw Christ standing on the right hand of God (Acts 7:55). Often Christ uttered statements such as, "I do nothing of myself; but as my Father hath taught me" (John 8:28).

Trinitarians sometimes quote John 10:30 to claim their view of the Godhead is valid: "I and my Father are one." This singular statement, taken out of context, is used to claim that the Godhead "is of one substance." However, in light of the foregoing scriptures, it must mean "one in purpose and unity." Later, John quotes the Savior's famous intercessory prayer, clarifying John 10:30 even further. Here Christ pleads with God the Father that His chosen apostles "all may be one; as thou, Father, art in me, and I in thee, that they also may be one in us" (John 17:21). Since Christ obviously was not praying to the Father for His disciples to become one person, but one in purpose, this declaration also applies to John 10:30.

Trinitarians also quote John 14:9: "He that has seen me has seen the Father." This scripture by itself could mean God and Jesus are the same, but again, in light of the foregoing scriptures, it means they are *alike,* not the same. It would be odd that Christ would compare Himself, possessing a physical body, to a father without body, parts and passions. In verses 24–28 of the same chapter in John, Christ says He and His father are separate.

21

Latter-day Saints do believe it is important to have a correct concept of deity in order to not just know about God, but to know God. Jesus prayed to His father: "This is life eternal, that they might know thee the only true God, and Jesus Christ, whom thou has sent" (John 17:3).

The dispute over the Godhead is not new to our day. Both before and after the Nicean council in A.D. 325, most Christians favored the view of a man named Arius, that Jesus was a being separate and distinct from the Father. This idea was favored by church fathers Ignatius, Hermes, Justin Martyr, Origen, and others. When Christianity became the state religion of the Roman Empire, bishops, who insisted on the Arian view of separateness, were replaced.

Further Readings: Hickenbotham (1995), 74–83; *EM* (1992), 552–555.

1.10. Why is the LDS Church called by some a sect or cult?

In our society, the words "sect" and "cult" usually have derogatory meanings. Usage of these terms by opponents is a way to degrade the LDS Church. A sect means "a religious body, especially one regarded as extreme or heretical that has separated from a larger denomination." Using *Webster's Ninth New Collegiate Dictionary* definition, Protestant groups are technically "sects," since they broke away from Catholicism. Early Christians were a sect because they broke away from Judaism. The Latter-day Saint Church is not an offshoot of any church. It is the Church of Christ from New Testament times that the Lord Jesus Christ restored to earth in our day. Thus, the term "sect" is completely inaccurate in defining Mormonism.

In current usage, the word "cult" usually means "a spurious, satanic, extreme, or radical group." Latter-day Saints are the complete opposite, opposing evil and fighting satanic influences. Leaders urge Latter-day Saints to react positively toward derogatory remarks in the same spirit as the Savior did at the time of His crucifixion: "Father, forgive them for they know not what they do" (Luke 23:34).

Further Readings: EM (1992), 1:345; Scharffs (1989), 356.

1.11. Is the LDS belief that humans can become gods biblical?

The precept is definitely biblical: "I have said, Ye are gods, and all of you are children of the most High" (Psalms 82:6). The Savior Himself taught this principle of the nature of man when His enemies tried to stone Him for claiming to be the Son of God. Christ rebuked His tormentors, quoting their own scripture, "Is it not written in your law, I said, Ye are gods?"

23

(John 10:34–35). The Lord then proclaimed this Old Testament scripture to be true. In the psalm cited by Jesus, Paul also testified: "We are the offspring of God" (Acts 17:29). Another scripture states: "We have had fathers of our flesh which corrected us, and we gave them reverence; shall we not much rather be in subjection unto the Father of spirits, and live" (Heb. 12:9). Paul and Hosea both said, "The spirit itself beareth witness with our spirit that we are the children of God" (Rom. 8:16; Hosea 1:10). The Apostle Peter declared, "Be ye partakers of the divine nature" (2 Pet. 1:4). John, the apostle, agreed, "We know that, when he shall appear, we shall be like him" (1 John 3:2).

We live in a society that emphasizes the degradation of mankind. Humans are defined in lowly terms. Deity, if believed in at all, is impersonal and abstract, such as a force of nature. Under such conditions, the heavens were opened while God and His Son Jesus Christ appeared to Joseph Smith and restored eternal truths. The historic event led to the establishment of The Church of Jesus Christ of Latter-day Saints. Ideas of deification were part of an eternal plan taught in holy writ since the world began.

The plan maintains a positive perception that the nature of man is good rather than evil, and that all humans are God's offspring. We are literally God's sons and daughters, created in His image with an unlimited potential of achieving growth, joy, eternal families, and perfection. These divine teachings were returned to earth for the blessing of all God's children through the first Latter-day Saint prophet, Joseph Smith.

Further Readings: EM (1992), 1369, 2:553, 2:677, 3:1230; Griffith (1989), 48.

1.12. Since Mormons believe there are many gods, aren't they polytheists?

Latter-day Saints are definitely not polytheistic. *Webster's Ninth New Collegiate Dictionary* defines polytheism as those who *worship* many gods. Although the LDS Church believes that there are many gods in the eternities, they do *not worship* many gods, which is completely different. The reality of many gods in the eternal realms is made clear in the Bible when it speaks of "God of gods" and "Lord of lords" as Paul and other prophets taught (Deut. 10:17; Ex. 15:11; 1 Cor. 8:5–6; Rev. 19:16).

Further Readings: Hickenbotham (1995), 5; Winward (1995), 32–33.

1.13. Is the LDS belief in a God that has a physical body anthropomorphic?

Anthropomorphism applies to those who ascribe human form and characteristics to God. At the Creation, God said, "Let us make man in our own image, after our own likeness . . . male and female created he them" (Gen. 1:26–27). Thus, there is a difference between God creating humans in His image and anthropomorphism, which means that humans have "ascribed human qualities to their God." So to be correct, anthropomorphism does not apply to LDS teachings. God also said, after the Fall, "The man is become as one of us" (Gen. 3:27), meaning that when Adam and Eve (with physical bodies) were created by God in His image, God patterned their bodies after His own. Latter-day Saints accept this Genesis scripture literally, whereas most Christians consider it figuratively.

Further evidence exists in the Bible to support the view that God has a physical body. One example is when Moses warned the children of Israel that they would be driven from their promised land and tempted to worship false gods who were "the work of men's hands, wood and stone, which neither see, nor hear, nor eat, nor smell" (Deut. 4:28). These gods would not be their true personal God who had the same attributes (hearing, eating, and smelling) that humans have. Another example is when God is speaking with Moses "face to face," which further underscores the LDS belief (Ex. 33:11).

These previous and following scriptures all support the idea that God has a body (certainly perfected and more glorious than the bodies mortals possess now). Following His resurrection, Jesus said, "Handle me and see; for a spirit hath not flesh and bones, as ye see me have" (Luke 24:39). The resurrected Savior (with a physical resurrected body) said, "He that hath seen me hath seen the Father." This indicates that Jesus and God are alike and that God too has a perfected physical body (John 14:9). The clearest scripture states, "The Father has a body of flesh and bones as tangible as man's; the Son also" (D&C 130:22).

Latter-day Saints do not intend to downgrade God, who is the epitome of glory and perfection, but LDS doctrine does greatly upgrade the common derogatory concept of man to first-class status. Mormons believe that humans, when they know they are God's offspring, are more likely to strive to keep His commandments and become more like Him.

Further Reading: Peterson (1995), 101.

1.14. Why don't Latter-day Saints use the cross as a symbol ?

Latter-day Saints do not have an aversion to the cross. They merely avoid emphasizing it. Not stressing the use of the cross is another of the many examples of Latter-day Saint teachings being in harmony with early Christianity. The Bible does not mention the cross as a symbol for Christianity. Several non-LDS scholars point out that the cross was not openly used as a Christian symbol in earlier times: "The early believers looked beyond the crucifixion to the Resurrection. Emphasis was not on the cross of suffering and humiliation, but on the promise of life

GILBERT SCHARFFS

with Christ" (Peterson and Ricks, 1992, 132). Using the cross as an icon of Christianity goes against the beliefs of those in Christ's day. The rare use of the word "cross" in the New Testament signifies that we, too, must bear our own crosses.

1.15. Are Latter-day Saints averse to Christ's suffering on the cross?

Latter-day Saints are most aware of Christ's infinite suffering. In weekly services, LDS members hear a priesthood holder pray that the congregation will partake of the sacrament of the Lord's Supper, "In remembrance of the blood of [Christ] which was shed for them."

The Book of Mormon also clarifies a controversial New Testament passage of Christ in the Garden of Gethsemane: "Being in agony . . . His sweat was as it were great drops of blood" (Luke 22:44). Some Christian writers claim the blood is merely a figurative expression, and it was really sweat that looked like blood in the dark, and thus not literally blood. Latter-day Saints have the words of an ancient American prophet who said that Christ would suffer "more than man can suffer, except it be unto death; for behold, *blood cometh from every pore*, so great shall be his anguish" (Mosiah 3:7; emphasis added).

Answering reporters in a press conference, LDS President Gordon B. Hinckley stated why the

Church does not emphasize the cross. After retelling the terrifying account of Christ's ordeal, President Hinckley said that Church members must never forget the excruciating suffering of the Lord. He added, "For us the cross is a symbol of a dying Christ, while our message is a declaration of the living Christ. The lives of our people must become the only meaningful expressions of our faith and, therefore, the symbol of our worship" (*Ensign*, May 1975, 93).

Further Reading: Peterson and Ricks (1992), 131–133.

1.16. Can Latter-day Saints claim they are "saved" as other Christians do?

Misunderstandings arise when the same words have different meanings to different people. This is especially true when it comes to a discussion of being "saved" (as in salvation). The following six points show where there are agreements and differences between Latter-day Saints and other Christians.

1. Most Christians (LDS and non-LDS) apparently agree that every aspect of salvation is enabled by Jesus Christ.

2. Most mainstream Christians and Latter-day Saints seem to agree that salvation includes resurrection for all mankind at some point after death: "As in Adam

29

all die, even so in Christ shall all be made alive" (1 Cor. 15:22). This aspect of salvation is unconditional. It does not require any effort, commitment, or even awareness of Jesus Christ. All humankind will be resurrected because of the Atonement of Jesus Christ.

3. When it comes to being saved from sin and going to heaven, differences in understanding begin to surface among Christian churches. Virtually all Christians believe Christ enables our return to heaven, but what is required to get there is where differences arise. To make this aspect of salvation possible Catholics stress Christian ritual (the Seven Sacraments), but they also believe personal effort is needed. Protestants stress faith in Christ, with some insisting that faith in Christ alone and accepting His love is sufficient. Latter-day Saints emphasize faith in Christ, rituals and works, including keeping God's commandments.

4. A further significant difference in salvation involves what happens to those who do not recognize and accept Christ. Most mainstream Christians believe such individuals will end up in a literal place called hell. They believe all those who don't believe as they do, both non-Christians and sometimes other Christians, are damned and lost. Latter day-Saints believe that hell is a physical location and an individual state of mind. It is remorse suffered for unrepented sin.

5. Latter-day Saints believe that just as all mankind is unconditionally resurrected (point 2), all mankind (sons of perdition excepted) will dwell in one of three kingdoms of glory in heaven. Christ had this in mind when He said, "in my Father's house are many mansions" (John 13:2). And Paul alluded to this when he spoke of a third heaven (2 Cor. 12:2). Paul also spoke of three kinds of resurrected bodies comparing their glory to the sun, moon, and stars (1 Cor. 15:40–42). Since the overwhelming majority of mankind (except the sons of perdition), will inherit one of the kingdoms, all mankind is saved in this sense. Latter-day Saint doctrine calls these the Three Degrees of Glory.

6. However, Mormon doctrine includes one other unique aspect of being saved. The top realm in heaven is called the Celestial Kingdom (See 1 Cor. 15:40). Within this kingdom of glory the highest division is referred to as a fulness of salvation. This level, also called exaltation, is based on merit. Besides good works, this kingdom is only achieved through the restored priesthood ordinances in the LDS Church. It requires temple covenants with God, including eternal marriage.

Here too, LDS doctrine provides for all mankind the opportunity to achieve this exaltation. Latter-day Saints accept literally the passages in the New Testament that state that after death and prior to

Christ's final judgement all mankind will dwell in a spirit world (See 1 Pet. 3:18–19). The Bible also states that those who did not have a chance to accept the gospel of Jesus Christ in mortality will have that opportunity in the spirit world (1 Pet. 4:6). The Bible makes it clear that earthly rites such as baptism are needed to enter the Kingdom of God (John 3:5; Mark 16:16; Acts 2:37–38). For this reason Latter-day Saints construct holy temples where they perform the necessary ordinances in behalf of the deceased, just as Christ's Atonement in Gethsemane and on the cross was done in behalf of all mankind.

Certainly God's official church would not be an exclusive group of elitists. Christ's church would teach the biblical doctrines of universal salvation and practice the teachings that enable both the living and deceased the opportunity for full salvation (exaltation). These biblical doctrines are only taught in The Church of Jesus Christ of Latter-day Saints, giving further evidence of the restoration of the fulness of the gospel.

1.17. What are the LDS views on faith and grace?

The LDS Church's Articles of Faith say that faith in the Lord Jesus Christ is the first principle of the gospel. If faith, which is part of the first LDS article of faith, were the only thing necessary for salvation, then Latter-day Saints would already be saved. Mormons do believe in the absolute necessity of faith and grace, but they also believe that works, righteousness, and essential rituals are necessary to please God. Latter-day Saints do not believe good works alone could ever save a person, but works are part of the process. By adding works, God would certainly not bar Latter-day Saints and many other religious people from salvation.

The Bible contains many passages on the necessity of faith in Jesus Christ and His grace. The same holy scriptures also have many verses requiring good works and keeping commandments. The necessity of ordinances (ritual) is also stressed in the Bible. Thus, concluding that we need faith, works, and essential saving ordinances is logical, honest, and biblical.

Those who insist that salvation requires faith alone ignore the many scriptures stating that God also requires good works. If ever there were a principle clearly taught in the Bible, it's the need to work at one's faith: "Faith without works is dead" (James 2:26) is one example. The Savior also said, "He that shall endure unto the end, the same shall be saved" (Mark 13:13), which means that salvation isn't earned in an instant, but requires constant effort.

Even passages that speak of faith are found in close proximity to verses that emphasize good works.

For example: "He that heareth my word, and believeth on him that sent me, hath everlasting life" (John 5:24). The same apostle also wrote in verse 29 of the same chapter that resurrection comes to those "that have done good" and "they that have done evil, unto the resurrection of damnation." To further stress this point John also wrote: "For this is the love of God, that we keep his commandments" and "All unrighteousness is sin" (1 John 5:3, 17).

Another verse that some claim means faith alone is when Paul said, "Christ Jesus came into the world to save sinners" (1 Tim. 1:15). It is incredulous to think that such verses exclude personal effort. In the same epistle Paul also said, "Be rich in good works" (1 Tim. 6:18; see also 1 Tim. 2:10; 5:10 and 2 Tim. 3:17).

Other words of Paul's in Romans 3:20, 28 are also used in an effort to prove that obeying laws for salvation are unnecessary: "By the deeds of the law there shall no flesh be justified in his sight." Paul is simply saying that the law is not enough. He makes this clear in verse 31 of the same chapter: "Do we then make void the law through faith? God forbid: yea, we establish the law." Paul explains that God would not give laws unless He expected us to keep them. The necessity of obeying God's laws is further emphasized when Paul says, "As many as have sinned in the law shall be judged by the law; For not the hearers of the law are just before God, but the *doers of the law* shall be justified" (Rom. 2:12–13; emphasis added). Paul, on another occasion, stressed the need for good works when he said God "will render to every man according to his deeds" (Rom. 2:6).

However, with all the scriptural emphasis on performance, Latter-day Saint doctrine emphatically teaches that work and essential rituals, as important as the scriptures say they are, are not enough. No one can have any aspect of salvation without Christ and His grace. That salvation and grace are an essential LDS belief is underscored in the Book of Mormon, which uses the word "grace" 35 times, for example, "It is by grace that we are saved, after all we can do" (2 Ne. 25:23; 2 Ne. 10:24 is similar).

Other Readings: EM (1992) 1:296, 2:560; Peterson and Ricks (1992), 137–148.

1.18. Where does the wealth of the LDS Church come from and is it justified?

Recently President Hinckley, responding to questions about the financial wealth of the Church, replied, "When all is said and done, the only real wealth of the Church is the faith of its people" ("Church Finances," www.lds.org). The people of the Church provide virtually all of the income by their tithes and offerings. However, since much is written about the Church's finances, further description is appropriate.

Recent articles and books estimate the assets of the Church comparable to *Fortune* magazine's 500 companies. *Time* magazine headlined a cover story titled "MORMONS, INC.," with a subheading "Latter-day Profits—The secrets of America's most prosperous religion" (4 August 1997). In 1999, the same authors expanded their article into a book called *Mormon America* (Ostling and Ostling (1999), 113–129). The writers were fair and accurate at times, but often wrong in their interpretations—especially concerning LDS finances.

A few years earlier, the *Arizona Republic* did a series of front page articles with a team of investigative reporters concerning the worth of The Church of Jesus Christ of Latter-day Saints. Just prior to that time, the national media had a field day reporting several financial scandals involving some churches in America. Newsmen from Phoenix jumped on the bandwagon in hopes of finding more exposés. They were looking for fraud and misuse of moneys in the LDS Church.

After an exhaustive search, the *Arizona Republic* concluded that although the LDS Church had vast wealth, they could find no improprieties in the management of funds. First, however, a reporter asked to see where the Church President Spencer W. Kimball lived. When he saw the modest home in a middle-class Salt Lake City neighborhood he remarked, "There is no scandal here."

President Gordon B. Hinckley has pointed out "that all of these are money-consuming assets and not money-producing assets. They do not produce financial wealth, but they do help to produce and strengthen Latter-day Saints" ("Church Finances," www.lds.org). He also said comparing the Church with normal businesses is not appropriate. The Church's schools, meetinghouses, welfare facilities, administrative offices, and temples do not earn money. Assets of business enterprises exist to make profits for owners and investors, which does not apply to the LDS Church nor most churches.

Businesses owned by the LDS Church, such as radio/TV stations, satellite facilities, and a newspaper, are justifiable since they help spread the message of the Church. Other religions often own media companies. Enterprises owned by the Church always pay taxes. Leaders state that the Church could only operate a few weeks if it had to rely on its investments.

The Church's business involvement in Utah came as a necessity. When the LDS pioneers came to the Salt Lake Valley, individual members began establishing commercial activities. Since most Latter-day Saints were impoverished, larger enterprises had to be financed by the Church because there was no one else to do it. When non-LDS merchants arrived and established retail stores, they had no rivalry and often charged excessive prices. The Church established its own competing businesses, including America's first department store, Zion's Cooperative Mercantile Institution (ZCMI), in order to bring about lower prices. Eventually, as more businesses were established by individual LDS and non-LDS merchants, the competition kept prices in check.

Over the years, the Church gradually divested itself of most businesses that were not directly involved with the furtherance of LDS purposes. Recently, the Church's Hotel Utah was converted to offices and a place for ward meetings. Renamed the Joseph Smith Memorial Building, it now also houses a theater for film productions about LDS history for visitors, and a family research area available for public use. In recent years, the Church-owned Zion's Bank and LDS hospitals were sold to private interests. In 1999, ZCMI's fourteen stores were sold to a national chain.

Many profits from the businesses the Church still owns are donated to non-LDS private and public schools, as well as to community and arts organizations. Non-LDS churches have expressed appreciation for contributions they receive for their building funds. On a global basis the Church also gives generous humanitarian financial aid and supplies to disaster-stricken areas. The United Way, the Red Cross and other groups benefit from LDS assistance. Such charitable organizations exist to support worthy causes and promote a better world. In addition to what the Church does, many members individually con-tribute to numerous charities. Some members also contribute directly to the LDS humanitarian fund, knowing that 100 percent of the money goes where disaster strikes.

CHAPTER TWO
The Bible is Basic

2.1. What are examples of the biblical basis of LDS doctrine not generally found in today's mainstream Christianity?

Much of the LDS doctrine that is found in the Bible is also practiced by mainstream Christianity. However, Latter-day Saints also believe in biblical teachings that are often missing from other Christian religions.

A. Nature of God

1. "The LORD your God is God of gods, and Lord of lords" (Deut. 10:7).

That there are many gods (lowercase *g*) and many lords (lowercase *l*) in the eternal realms is clear in the Bible. It is also obvious that there is only one God of this earth (spelled with a capital G in this verse). Paul agreed: "For though there be many that are called gods . . . to us there is but one God" (1 Cor. 8:5–6). Few Christians, besides Latter-day Saints, believe there are many gods in heavenly realms (see Psalms 97:9; 136:2–3). That there is only one God for this earth is also made clear in passages such as Isaiah 45:5.

2. "The Lord spake unto Moses face to face, as a man speaketh unto his friend" (Ex. 33:11).

Latter-day Saints interpret this verse literally and believe when the Bible says "God created man in his own image," meaning humans have similar attributes to God (Gen. 1:27; 5:1–2; 9:6). Most religions teach that such expressions in the Bible are only figurative. They reason that since the human mind cannot relate to an abstract God, writers of the Bible ascribed human qualities to God. Latter-day Saints believe it is easier, and biblically correct, to believe in a God that is not abstract in the first place. If "face to face" is used as an understandable substitute for the real abstract "God," some have argued that the Bible is party to deception. Furthermore, the Old Testament writer supported Genesis 1:27 when he reported that when Moses, and Aaron . . . and seventy of the Elders of Israel saw God, they described a paved sapphire stone "under his feet" (Ex. 24:9–10). On another occasion the biblical writer describes the detailed attributes of God as able to see, hear, eat, and smell (Deut. 4:27–29). Latter-day Saints believe that knowing we are of God's image and likeness makes it easier to obey, worship, and relate to Him. Mormons believe this is what the Apostle John meant when he said

"This is life eternal, that they might know thee the only true God, and Jesus Christ, whom thou has sent" (John 17:3). This is also what God meant when, in the first of the Ten Commandments, He said, "Thou shalt have no other gods before me" (Ex. 20:3).

3. Jesus is the God of the Old Testament (John 8:56–59).

When Jesus claimed that He knew the Abraham in their scriptures (Old Testament), the crowd became angry, saying, "Thou art not yet fifty years old, and thou hast seen Abraham? Jesus said unto them . . . Before Abraham was, I am." The crowd then cast stones at Him because Christ was claiming to be "I AM," the God of the Old Testament. In the Old Testament, God had said unto Moses "I AM THAT I AM" and He said, "Thus shalt thou say unto the children of Israel, I AM hath sent me unto you . . . this is my name forever" (Ex.3:14–15). John also says Christ was God of the earth (John 1:1–14). In verses 1–13 it speaks of the God who made this world as "the Word." And in verse 14 it clarifies "the Word" as Christ: "And the Word was made flesh, and dwelt among us, (and we beheld his glory, the glory as of the only begotten of the Father)." Paul refers to the Israelites in the Old Testament drinking of "that spiritual Rock that followed them: and that Rock was Christ" (1 Cor. 10:4).

4. Jesus at times may be referred to as "Father" (Isaiah 9:6).

"For unto us a child is born, unto us a son is given . . . his name shall be called Wonderful, Counsellor, The mighty God, The everlasting Father" (Isaiah 9:6). Christians believe this verse, immortalized by Handel's *Messiah* oratorio, as referring to the coming of Christ. Latter-day Saints maintain this verse sanctions the use of Father in referring to Christ at times.

5. "Is not this the carpenter, the son of Mary, the brother of James, and Joses, and of Juda, and Simon? and are not his sisters here with us?" (Mark 6:3).

In spite of such verses, a concept called Immaculate Conception is part of today's mainstream Christianity. This doctrine is not taught in the Bible. The immaculate conception doctrine states that Mary never had any other children nor even marital relations with her husband Joseph. Latter-day Saints agree that Christ's mother was a virgin, but after the birth of Jesus she had other children by her mortal husband, Joseph.

6. God said, "Let us make man in our image" (Gen. 1:26).

Sometime later, God again said "Man is become as one of us" (Gen. 3:22). The plural "us" argues for more than one God. Latter-day Saints differ from most Christians because they are convinced that the Bible clearly teaches three separate Gods in the Godhead. (For further discussion on the Trinity see chapter one, question 1.9.) For further reading on some of the many scriptures that support the LDS "separateness" position, see Acts 7:44; John 5:19; 5:30; 5:45; 6:32; 6:38; 7:16; 7:29; 8:28; 8:29; 8:43; 10:37; 13:16; 14:24; 14:28; 15:21; 15:10; 16:3 16:16; 17:20–21.

7. "Handle me, and see; for a spirit hath not flesh and bones, as ye see me have" (Luke 24:39).

So spake Jesus to His disciples after His crucifixion. "With great power gave the apostles witness of the resurrection" of Christ (Acts 4:33). Latter-day Saints feel that after all the effort Jesus put forth to let His followers see and feel His resurrected body, He did not shed that resurrected body, when He returned to His Father in Heaven. The scriptures do not even hint that He does not have a perfected resurrected body today. The Trinitarian concept of mainstream Christianity does not permit Jesus to have a body after His Ascension into heaven. Latter-day Saints unequivocally proclaim that both Christ and God the Father have glorified resurrected bodies as the Bible teaches.

B. God Works Through Priesthood and Prophets

8. "Surely the Lord God will do nothing, but he revealeth his secret unto his servants the prophets" (Amos 3:7).

Paul said prophets were necessary until "we all come to a unity of faith" (Eph. 4:11–13). Aside from Latter-day Saints, belief in modern prophets is rare. (Other scriptures which speak of the necessity of prophets include Luke 1:70; Acts 3:21; Eph. 2:20; 3:5; Jer. 7:25.)

9. The Lord gave unto man "the covenant of an everlasting priesthood" (Num. 25:12–13).

Priesthood is mentioned nearly two dozen times in the Bible. Peter referred to church members as "a chosen generation, a royal priesthood" (1 Peter 2: 5, 9). Chapters 5–7 of Hebrews speak of the necessity of priesthood, as does Exodus 40:15. Catholics and Mormons stress priesthood. Some Protestants have a "priesthood of all believers," which means anyone can take priesthood upon themselves. This practice is not mentioned in scripture. Actually, the Bible says, "No man taketh this honor upon himself, but he that is called of God, as was Aaron" (Heb. 5:4).

10. The household of God is "built on the foundation of the apostles and prophets" (Eph. 2:19).

As part of the restoration of the gospel, these priesthood offices were restored when The Church of Jesus Christ of Latter-day Saints was organized.

11. Christ "gave some, apostles; and some, prophets; . . . for the edifying of the body of Christ:

Till we all come in the unity of the faith" (Eph. 4:11–13).

Since the world does not have a unity of faith, these priesthood offices are still essential today in Christ's Church, as this scripture declares. LDS leadership is patterned after the New Testament prototype. Since Christ lived a perfect life, as most Christians believe, Latter-day Saints also believe His pattern of organization was perfect and should be followed.

12. There are two priesthoods "after the order of Melchizedec" and "after the order of Aaron" (Heb. 7:11).

Those few churches that speak of some kind of priesthood do not identify it by the names used by biblical writers: Melchizedek and Aaronic. These two priesthoods are an essential part of the LDS Church: "Thou art a priest forever after the order of Melchizedek" (Psalms 110:4). This verse says that the Melchizedek priesthood would always be part of God's church: "Melchizedec King of Salem, was the priest of the most high God" (Gen. 14:18).

13. Every high priest "among men is ordained . . . in things pertaining to God" (Heb. 5:1).

Although mentioned 75 times in the Bible, high priests are rarely part of Christian churches. The apostle Paul speaks of high priests being "holy, harmless . . . and made separate from sinners" (Heb. 7:26). They are an important leadership position in the LDS Church.

14. "Know that the Lord hath set apart him that is godly" (Psalms 4:3).

As far as I have been able to determine, only Latter-day Saints use the term "set apart" in calling eligible members to church leadership positions.

15. Ye shall "keep mine ordinances, to walk therein: I am the Lord your God"(Lev. 18:4).

The word "ordinance(s)" is repeated 61 times in the Bible, but the word is not common in Judeao/Christian terminology today. The biblical word "ordinance" is used often in the LDS Church to describe a sacred ritual. Many churches perform rituals and use the word "rites," (which appears only once in the Bible) or the word "sacrament," which never appears in the Bible.

16. "Moses . . . laid his hands upon [Joshua], and gave him a charge, as the Lord commanded" (Num. 27:22–23).

Later, this pattern of laying on of hands in delegating authority and bestowing blessings was mentioned again in the Bible: "Joshua . . . was full of the spirit of wisdom; for Moses had laid his hands upon him . . . and did as the Lord commanded" (Deut. 34:9). While filming *The Ten Commandments*, Cecile B. DeMille asked LDS president David O. McKay how to portray this incident. The LDS president pointed out these verses, and the epic movie depicted it in that way. In the New Testament, little children were brought to Christ "and he put his hands on them and blessed them" (Mark 10:13,16). When Christ's disciples were called, it was done with the laying on of hands (See Acts 6:6). This procedure was also used to bestow the Holy Ghost on new converts (See Acts 8:17). Numerous other examples are found in the Holy Bible (See Lev. 16:2; Ex. 29:10; Heb. 6:2; 1 Tim. 4–14; Acts 8:17). However, this biblical pattern, used extensively by Latter-day Saints, is not as common in mainstream Christianity today.

17. "Is any sick among you? let him call for the elders of the church; and let them pray over him, anointing him with oil in the name of the Lord" (James 5:14).

This ordinance of anointing with consecrated oil and blessing the sick by the laying on of hands of elders occurs often in The Church of Jesus Christ of Latter-day Saints. The word "oil" combined with some form of the word "anoint" appears 43 times in the Bible. A well-known verse reads: "The Lord is my shepherd; I shall not want; he maketh me lie down in

green pastures . . . thou anointest my head with oil;
my cup runneth over" (Psalms 23:1, 5).

C. A Temple of the Lord is Essential.

18. "The Lord is in his holy temple" and Christ's
followers continue to worship "daily with one accord
in the temple" (Psalms 11:4; Acts 2:46).

A temple was the Church's second structure, completed in Kirtland, Ohio, in 1936, and the Nauvoo,
Illinois Temple was restored in 2002. Temples are vital to
Latter-day Saints, with more than a hundred dedicated
around the world when the twenty-first century began.

19. "The king went up into the house of the
Lord" (2 Kings 23:2).

Usage of "house of the Lord" appears 213 times
in the Bible and is synonymous with the word "temple." The phrase appears on LDS temples today.

20. "David . . . washed, and anointed himself, and
changed his apparel, and came into the house of the
Lord, and worshiped" (2 Sam. 12:20).

This pattern is similar to procedures followed
today in Latter-day Saint temples.

21. "Thou shalt make holy garments for Aaron . . .
that he may minister unto me in the priest's office"
(Ex. 28:2–3; 40:13).

Temple-worthy Latter-day Saints wear sacred garments as reminders of covenants made with God.

22. "God said, This is the token of the covenant which I make between me and you" (Gen. 9:12).

Symbolic tokens representing covenants made with the Lord are part of LDS temple worship.

23. "Thou shalt be called by a new name" (Isaiah 62:2; See also Rev. 3:12).

The new name mentioned in the Old and New Testaments is part of the LDS temple procedure.

24. "Behold, I will send you Elijah the prophet . . . and he shall turn the heart of the fathers to the children, and the heart of the children to their fathers" (Malachi 4:5–6).

An important part of Jewish ritual is in anticipation of this event, which is referred to in the closing words of the Old Testament. Latter-day Saint scripture records the coming of Elijah on April 3, 1836, to the first LDS temple in Kirtland, Ohio, in fulfillment of this biblical prophecy. At this time, Elijah restored keys for temple and genealogy work to Joseph Smith and Oliver Cowdery. This made it possible for LDS members to perform vicarious ordinances for deceased relatives, such as baptism, in temples dedicated for that purpose (D&C 110:13–16).

25. "Else what shall they do which are baptized for the dead, if the dead rise not at all? why are they then baptized for the dead?" (1 Cor. 15:29)

Some Bible translations use the more precise term "in behalf of the dead" (Goodspeed translation). Several historical sources make it clear that this was practiced in the early Christian church. "It was 'those apostles and teachers' of the first generation according to the Shepherd of Hermas, who 'went down living into the water' in behalf of those who had died" (Hugh Nibley, "Baptism for the Dead in Ancient Times," *Improvement Era,* Feb. 1949, 109–110; also cited in Griffeth, 1989, 129). One of the main activities in LDS temples is baptisms for the dead.

26. "God put into mine heart to gather together . . . the people, that they might be reckoned by genealogy" (Neh. 7:5).

Genealogy is mentioned 28 times in the Bible, mostly to identify families and those who belonged to certain tribes. It is essential to LDS theology and practice, because it identifies ancestors, so that the proxy ordinances may be performed in LDS temples.

27. "A book of remembrance was written" for the Lord (Malachi 3:16).

Latter-day Saints are encouraged to keep a book of remembrance containing their history and family records. This record will also have future significance involving the temple (D&C 128:24).

D. Other Biblical Doctrines and Practices

28. "Will a man rob God? Yet ye have robbed me. But ye say, Wherein have we robbed thee? In tithes and offerings" (Malachi 3:8-10).

Latter-day Saints are encouraged to give ten percent of their earnings as tithes. While they are not the only religion to preach this concept, most Christian churches and Jews do not stress this biblical teaching that has 31 biblical references.

29. "He shall be great in the sight of the Lord, and shall drink neither wine nor strong drink" (Luke 1:15).

The Old Testament gives similar advice: "Drink not wine nor strong drink" (Judges 13:4). The Bible, as we have it today, gives us mixed signals on the use of alcoholic beverages and at times seems to condone the use of wine, but the wise person will follow the higher law as detailed in the Bible. Numerous passages condemn the use of intoxicating drinks. In Proverbs we read, "Wine is a mocker, strong drink is raging: and whosoever is deceived thereby is not wise" (Prov. 20:1). Also in Daniel it says, "Daniel . . . would not defile himself with . . . the king's wine" (Daniel 1:18). Paul taught that a bishop must not be given "to wine"

(Titus 1:7). Latter-day Saints are expected not to use alcoholic beverages as part of their strict health code.

30. "Give yourself to fasting and prayer" (1 Cor. 7:5).

The Lord said, "Turn ye even to me with all your heart and with fasting" (Joel 2:12). When Jesus faced the important decision to choose His twelve apostles, He first fasted (Matt. 4). Latter-day Saints today also fast for special purposes when spiritual strength is needed, as well as a monthly fast.

31. "Walk in the Spirit, and ye shall not fulfil the lust of the flesh" (Gal. 5:16).

The Lord condemns both heterosexual and homosexual sins. The Savior warned, "Whomsoever looketh on a woman to lust after her hath committed adultery with her already in his heart" (Matt. 5:28). Paul taught, "Be not deceived: neither fornicators . . . nor adulterers, nor effeminate, nor abusers of themselves with mankind" (1 Cor. 6:9). On another occasion Paul said, "For this cause God gave them up unto vile affections: for even their women did change the natural use into that which is against nature: And likewise also the men, leaving the natural use of the woman, burned in their lust one toward another; men with men working that which is unseemly" (Romans 1:26–27). The same concept of sexual purity was also taught in the Old Testament: "There shall be no whore of the daughters of Israel, nor a sodomite of the sons of Israel" (Deut. 23:17).

32. "I would they were even cut off which trouble you" (Gal. 5:12).

Throughout biblical history, unrepentant sinners were expelled from the main body of worshipers. God certainly expects His people to be role models for others. "Be thou an example of the believers" (1 Tim. 4:12). Latter-day Saint disciplinary councils are events where love is the foremost concern and where sanctions against those who commit serious sins begin with a period of probation. Church leaders work long hours trying to help offending members, and professional counseling might also be recommended. If a person continues to engage in serious sins, disfellowshipment or excommunication could be the verdict of a Church council. Excommunication is reserved for the most serious offenses, and is almost certainly the verdict when it involves a member in a Church leadership position.

Disfellowshipping or excommunication does not mean the Church has turned its back on sinners. Leaders continue to labor with such individuals, if possible, to help with their problems. Often Church disciplinary actions bring about repentance and change in the lives of the offenders, and those who had their Church membership revoked often return to the Church in full standing.

33. "Jesus saith unto him, get thee hence, Satan (Matt. 4:10).

Dozens of scriptures in the Bible speak of Satan and the other names he is called, such as the devil. Some Christians think Satan in the Bible is figurative and not real. Other Christians, including Latter-day Saints, teach that he is real.

34. "Arise, O Lord God . . . and let thy saints rejoice in goodness" (2 Chron. 6:41).

There are ninety-eight usages of the word *saint(s)* scattered throughout the Bible, referring to followers of the Lord. Paul wrote "Unto the church of God, which is at Corinth, to them that are sanctified in Christ Jesus, called to be *saints*, with all that in every place call upon the name of Jesus Christ our Lord" (1 Cor. 1:2). The same apostle taught, "For God is not the author of confusion, but of peace, as in all churches of *saints*" (1 Cor. 14:33). The Old Testament often uses the word *saints* as when the psalmist said, "Praise ye the Lord. Sing unto the Lord a new song, and praise in the congregation of the *saints*" (Ps. 149:1). Thus, by having *Saints* in its title, The Church of Jesus Christ of Latter-day Saints is following the biblical pattern.

35. "I knew a man in Christ . . . such an one caught up to the third heaven" (2 Cor. 12:2, RSV).

Latter-day Saints believe there are three main divisions in heaven, as the verse suggests. LDS doctrine also includes subsections in these three heavens which ties in with the statement made by the Savior: "In my Father's house are many mansions . . . I go to prepare a place for you" (John 14:2). Another verse germane to the LDS position says, "The heaven and heaven of heavens cannot contain thee" (1 Kings 8:27). Latter-day Saints call these three heavens (kingdoms) celestial, terrestrial and telestial. This is similar to Paul's description of the resurrection: "There are also celestial bodies, and bodies terrestrial . . . There is one glory of the sun, and another glory of the moon, and another glory of the stars: for one star differeth from another star in glory. So also is the resurrection of the dead" (1 Cor. 15:40–42). Most Christians believe in only one heaven.

36. "Remember the Sabbath day, to keep it holy" (Ex. 20:8).

In a world where Sabbath observance is rare, Latter-day Saints are encouraged to keep this fourth commandment. It is a day to attend church, visit those with special needs, study the scriptures and be at home with the family.

37. Jesus said, "Unless a man is born of the water and the Spirit he cannot enter into the Kingdom of God (John 3:5).

Most Christians believe baptism is essential; others however, do not believe it is necessary. The above scripture makes it clear that being born of Christ involves a baptism by water and a separate spiritual ritual.

38. John answered . . . I baptize you with water; but one mightier than I (Jesus) . . . shall baptize you with the Holy Ghost" (Luke 3:16).

Being born of the Spirit involves laying on of hands to bestow the Holy Ghost upon Church members. The apostles performed this rite of bestowing the Holy Ghost by the laying on of hands (Acts 8:18). When Paul found some followers of Christ who had only received a water baptism he "laid his hands upon them, [and] the Holy Ghost came on them" (Acts 19:1–6). Most Christians have some form of baptism, but only Latter-day Saints have an ordinance that bestows the Holy Ghost by the laying on of hands.

E. The Noble Heritage and Destiny of the Human Race.

39. "The spirit shall return unto God who gave it" (Eccl. 12:7).

Since this verse indicates that we return to the presence of God, we must have been there before birth. The

Lord also made it clear that we had a premortal existence when He said to the prophet Jeremiah: "Before I formed thee in the belly I knew thee; and before thou camest forth out of the womb I sanctified thee" (Jer. 1:4–5). That we existed before this mortal life is learned from Job when the Lord also asked, "Where wast thou when I laid the foundations of the earth? . . . and all the sons of God shouted for joy?" (Job 38:4–7). Paul supports the concept that we lived with our Heavenly Father when he taught, since we "had fathers of our flesh which corrected us, and we gave them reverence: shall we not be in subjection unto the Father of spirits, and live?" (Heb. 12:9).

Probably the best teaching of our existence in a life before this life is shown when Christ's disciples asked Him whether a certain blind man or his parents had sinned in a previous life. Jesus' reply confirmed premortal existence when He said, "Neither hath this man sinned, nor his parents" (John 9:2–3). Latter-day Saints and Zoroastrians are virtually alone in believing in the premortal existence of humans.

40. "Adam's transgression" and "the woman's transgression" (Rom. 5:14; 1 Tim. 2:14).

Most of Christianity considers Adam and Eve vile sinners and the Fall a great tragedy. Latter-day Saints believe it was a necessary step in order to have a mortal experience, which was part of God's plan for humankind. It is true, Adam and Eve were forbidden by God to eat of the "tree of knowledge of good and evil" (Gen. 2:17). In the creation account in Genesis, neither the words "sin" nor "transgression" are used to describe the Fall. Instead of "sin," Latter-day Saints use the milder term "transgression," which the apostle Paul used in the above passages. (See the second article of faith). However, eating the forbidden fruit did have consequences: Adam and Eve were expelled from the nonstress Garden of Eden into a world of death, struggle, and suffering (Gen. 3:16–19). Latter-day Saints believe these consequences were desirable, because the Lord said, "Cursed is the ground *for thy sake*" (Gen. 3:17; emphasis added). Latter-day Saint doctrine teaches that the Fall was part of God's plan and was necessary for mankind to have a mortal experience where they could gain experience, be tested, have children, and progress to become like God. Gen. 3:22 states: "And the Lord God said, Behold, *the man is become as one of us*, to know good and evil" (emphasis added)

41. God said, "Be fruitful, and multiply, and replenish the earth" (Gen. 1:28).

Latter-day Saints do *not* believe the Fall was a tragic mistake or had anything to do with sexual sin, as some Christians believe. Since God first commanded them to have children, it was not possible to sin in this regard. Latter-day Saints believe that since this commandment to have children was given first, before they were placed in the Garden of Eden, it thus was a more important commandment to keep in the eternal scheme of things. Latter-day doctrine teaches that the commandments were not actually contradictory. The command not to eat of the fruit of knowledge of good and evil in the Garden of Eden was to initiate the principle of free will. Mortality, with all of its risks and problems, had to be a willful choice. Adam and Eve, choosing mortality, acted in behalf of all their descendants who would follow them coming to earth. The commandment pertained to the garden. Latter-day Saints believe breaking a commandment in the garden was necessary to introduce mortality in order to learn good and evil and have children.

42. "Neither is the man without the woman, neither is the woman without the man, in the Lord" (1 Cor. 11:11).

Paul's statement makes it clear that marriage is ordained of God. We also read in scripture "What therefore God has joined together, let not man put asunder (Matt. 19:5–6; Mark 10:9). Other scriptures also suggest the eternal nature of marriage: "I know that, whatsoever God doeth, it shall be for ever" (Eccl. 3:14). Christ taught this idea when He told

His apostles, "Whatsoever thou shalt bind on earth, shall be bound in heaven" (Matt. 16:19). The Savior's statement certainly suggests that authorized rites (such as marriage) would be binding in heaven.

Some claim the Bible says there will be no marriage in heaven. They refer to Mark 12:25, which states resurrected individuals "neither marry, nor are given in marriage." This verse does not say there won't be any marriage in heaven, only that marriages will not be performed there. Latter-day Saints build temples, which are dedicated as houses of the Lord where marriages for the living, and by proxy for the dead, are performed.

43. "Children are an heritage of the Lord: and the fruit of the womb is his reward" (Ps. 127:3).

Again we see the importance and sacredness of life. The Lord said to Moses at the time He gave the Ten Commandments: "If men strive, and hurt a woman with a child, so that her fruit depart from her . . . he shall be surely punished" (Ex. 21:22).

44. "We are the offspring of God" (Acts 17:29).

Latter-day Saints believe these words spoken by Paul in his famous Mars Hill sermon in Athens. These verses and others reveal each human's divine legacy and future potential. Jesus also referred to mankind as being of God's species when He said, "Ye are gods, and all of you are children of the most High" (Ps. 82:6; See also John 10:34). Most Christian churches interpret these verses to be dealing with man's divine heritage figuratively (see chapter one, question 1.12).

For anyone to say that Latter-day Saints are not biblical is a gross misunderstanding. Further study will reveal more biblical teachings that Latter-day Saints believe which many Christians do not.

2.2. How do Latter-day Saints justify having additional scripture to the Bible?

Called as a prophet by the Lord, it is proper that Joseph Smith would add new revelations as previous prophets did. Humankind certainly deserves and needs as much help from God in our day as the ancients did. "Surely the Lord God will do nothing, but he revealeth his secret unto his servants the prophets" (Amos 3:7).

Most Christians believe in a closed canon, meaning that the Bible should not be added to. Since Latter-day Saints have scriptures in addition to the Bible, this opposes mainstream Christian thought. In defense of the LDS position, a brief review of how the Bible was compiled argues for the LDS view of an open canon. The Bible itself refers to several sacred books that became lost and never found their way into today's canonized Bible. The book of Shemiah the prophet (2 Chr. 12:15) and the sayings of the

seers (2 Chr. 33:19) are two examples. In 1
Corinthians 5:9 Paul refers to an earlier epistle to the
Corinthians. (See also Ex. 24:7; Num. 21:14; Josh.
10:13; 1 Chr. 29:29; 2 Chr. 9:29; 13:22; 20:34 and
Col. 4:16). If these books were available today, they
might be considered scripture.

Books within the Bible have been added and
subtracted in the early centuries after Christ's death at
the whim of councils. Biblical scholar John A.
Tvedtness has pointed out that "the earliest known
listings of New Testament books accepted by
Christians is the Muratorian Canon, ca. A.D.
160–170. It lists most books in our present New
Testament, but excludes 2 Peter and 3 John. It was
not until 365 A.D. that the 27 books of our present
New Testament were in an official list prepared by
Athanasius, Bishop of Alexandria. He left out some
early Christians' favorite books, such as the Epistle of
Barnabas, The Didache, 1 Clement, the apocalypse of
Peter and the Shepherd of Hermes" (unpublished
paper in author's file). Thus we see that the content of
the Bible has fluctuated over the centuries.

In light of the foregoing changes in the Bible, it
should not be considered strange for Latter-day
Saints to believe in an open canon (additional scripture), since that is what the Bible was for centuries. In
fact, Latter-day Saints believe the Bible makes reference to the Book of Mormon. In the Bible Jesus said

there were "other sheep" He would visit that were not of that fold. One such visit by Christ to Book of Mormon people states they are the ones He spoke of in the Holy Land (3 Ne. 11–24).

Latter-day Saints are not the first to claim scripture in addition to the Bible. Just as early Christians added the New Testament to the older scriptures they possessed, Latter-day Saints are continuing to add to the two biblical testaments. The Book of Mormon, as its subtitle suggests, is an addition to the Bible as "another testament of Jesus Christ."

Further Readings: Griffith (1989), 85–87; Winwood (1995), 67, 65.

2.3. Does not the Bible itself forbid additional scripture?

The apostle John said, "If any man shall add unto these things, God shall add unto him the plagues that are written in this book" (Rev. 22:18). Some claim that this verse at the end of the New Testament means nothing should be added to the Bible. A similar verse in the Old Testament, Deuteronomy 4:2, says essentially the same thing as John's preceding quote from the book of Revelation. Thus one could claim that any books beyond the book of Deuteronomy are invalid. John, the author of Revelation, was speaking only about *his* writings. He had no idea that hundreds of years later his manuscript would be placed at the end of a volume of books called the New Testament. The word Bible means collection of books, not one book. Some areas of early Christianity did not accept the epistles of John or the book of Revelation. Some New Testament books were written after the book of Revelation, which would make them invalid if that book marked the end of scripture.

Further Readings: Griffith (1989), 93–95; Hickenbotham (1995), 178–182.

2.4. Since the Bible is the "Word," is it not the final authority for God's truth?

The Bible itself makes no claim to be the complete word of God. The apostle John calls Christ "*the* Word," not a book. "The Word was made flesh, and dwelt among us, (and we beheld his glory, the glory as of the only begotten of the Father, full of grace and truth")(John 1:14).

Christ, in His intercessory prayer, asks His Father in Heaven to sanctify His followers, "through thy truth; thy word is truth" (John 17:17). Some who believe that the Bible alone is the word of God quote this verse. The interpretation does not take into consideration Paul's teaching that "the kingdom of God is not in word, but in power" (1 Cor. 4:20). Latter-day Saints believe the Bible contains the word of God, but that the Bible alone is not the word of God.

Further Reading: Peterson and Ricks (1992), 117–128.

2.5. Do Latter-day Saints accept the Bible as infallible and inerrant as other Christians do?

Only some Christians believe the Bible is infallible. Latter-day Saints believe "the Bible is true as far as it is translated correctly" (eighth article of faith). In divinity schools, much time is spent in the field of higher biblical criticism. These studies deal with problems in Bible translations.

1. Some examples of discrepancies between versions of the Bible are:

A. In the King James version and some other translations of the Bible, Job, speaking of the time after death, says, "In my flesh will I see God" (Job 19:26). Some translations say that Job *"without"* his flesh would see God after the resurrection (*American Baptist Publication Society* and *The Modern Language Bible* are two such editions). The Hebrew Bible states, "from my flesh I will see God." This vague expression could mean "from within my flesh" or "from without my flesh."

B. 1 Samuel 6:18 in the King James version says the Lord slew 50,070 Philistines when they captured the ark of the covenant. The Septuagint, the Revised Standard Version, and other translations, say it was only seventy.

2. Some contradictions within the same text.

A. It is recorded in 1 Chronicles 21:5 that David's census reported a total of 1,500,070 men in the military; in 2 Sam. 24:9 the total given is only 1,300,000. 2 Sam.10:18 reads 700 chariots; 1 Chron. 19:18 speaks of the same situation as 7,000 chariots. 2 Kings gives the age of Jehoiachin on ascension as eighteen; 2 Chron. 26:9 says the age was eight.

B. John 3:22 says Jesus baptized; in the next chapter, John 4:2, still speaking about the same event it states, "Jesus himself baptized not."

C. In Matthew 27:9 it speaks of the prophecy made by *Jeremiah* regarding 30 pieces of silver; however *Zechariah* made the prediction (See Zech. 11:12). In the story of how the disciples plucked the ears of corn and so broke the Sabbath, Mark 2:26 refers to David in the days of the priest Abiathar; however, it was Ahimelch who was the priest then (See 1 Sam. 21:6).

D. When Luke 18:35–43 reports the story of Jesus healing the blind at Jericho, only one man is mentioned; in Matt. 20:29–34 two men are spoken of.

E. Mark 10:37 explains that James and John asked the Savior if they could sit "one on thy right hand, and the other on thy left hand, in thy glory;" however, Matthew 2:20–29 has the mother of the brothers James and John making the request.

F. Acts 9:7 states that "the men which journeyed with [Paul] stood speechless, hearing a voice;" however in Acts 29:9 Paul states those with him "heard not the voice."

Some believe the Bible is perfect. Others feel it is a myth. Latter-day Saints disagree with these extreme views. We love the Bible, study it, and proclaim it is remarkably accurate, but recognize some errors. Omissions, contradictions and imperfections in today's Bibles do not diminish the greatness of the Holy Bible or the work of the Lord. These problems might not exist if we had the original texts available. *Further Readings:* Griffith (1994), 73–75, *EM* (1992), 1:112; Peterson and Ricks (1992), 117–128.

2.6. Is it true that Latter-day Saints have their own version of the Bible?

Latter-day Saints consider the King James Version their official Bible in English speaking countries. In recent years, the Church has published greatly enhanced editions of its scriptures, including the King James Bible in 1982. There was not a single change in the Bible text, but footnotes were added, including cross-references to other LDS scriptures. In 1982, the Layman's National Bible committee presented to The Church of Jesus Christ of Latter-day Saints an award for "Outstanding Service to the Bible Cause." This honor was in recognition of the new LDS edition of the King James Bible.

Further Reading: EM (1992) 1:111.

2.7. Did Joseph Smith rewrite the Bible?

With divine inspiration, Joseph Smith revised many passages in the King James Bible as he studied it. Most of the significant passages are found in the footnotes of the 1982 edition of the King James Bible that the Church now uses. Joseph Smith's revision, published by the Reorganized Church of Jesus Christ of Latter-day Saints (now called Community of Saints), is available in LDS bookstores. At times, Latter-day Saints use it and other translations to gain insight to their scripture study. Since Joseph Smith did not complete his revision, and because of the basic accuracy and widespread usage of the King James translation, it is the Church's Bible of preference.

Further Readings: Peterson (1995), 97–98; *EM* (1992), 2:763–798, 4:1709.

2.8. Are the other LDS scriptures more important to Church members than the Bible?

The Bible is central to LDS doctrine and might be considered the bedrock of Mormonism. Other books that Latter-day Saints accept as scripture are supplemental to the Bible. When publishing all four of its canonized scriptures in one volume, the LDS Church always places the Bible first, showing its importance. Joseph Smith said of the Bible: "He who reads oftenest will like it best, and he who is acquainted with it, will know the hand [of the Lord]" (*Teachings,* 56). This was true in Joseph Smith's own life. It was a passage from the Bible that prompted him on his prayerful quest to find religious answers: "If any of you lack wisdom, let him ask of God" (James 1:5). When the Angel Moroni appeared to Joseph Smith, telling him the whereabouts of the Book of Mormon plates, he quoted several biblical passages, showing the importance of the Bible to the restoration of the gospel.

The Book of Mormon itself often attests to the basic truthfulness of the Bible and Jesus Christ: "For behold, this [Book of Mormon] is written with the intent that ye may believe [The Bible]" (Mormon 7:9; see also 1 Ne. 13:39–40). The introduction page of the Book of Mormon describes itself as "a volume of holy scripture comparable to the Bible." It continues to explain that the Book of Mormon contains "as does the Bible, the fulness of the everlasting gospel." In modern scripture the Lord told Joseph Smith, "Teach the principles of my gospel, which are in the Bible and the Book of Mormon" (D&C 42:12). LDS apostle Bruce R. McConkie, who wrote several vol-

umes about the New Testament, said, "The Bible is
the book of books" (McConkie (1966), 79).

Further Reading: Scharffs (1989), 159–160.

CHAPTER THREE
Book of Mormon Essentials

3.1. What do we learn about Christ in the Book of Mormon that is not found in the Bible?

Since the Book of Mormon people are of biblical descent, the "new world" scripture teaches many of the same principles as the "old world" Bible. The Savior made several visitations to His people in America, as recorded in the Book of Mormon. This is another reason one would expect many similarities between the two volumes. However, the Bible is missing many passages as well as complete books, and contains some translation errors. Those who study the Bible come to different interpretations, which results in many different churches. There is much in the Book of Mormon that clarifies vague, missing, and disputed passages, as well as contains unique concepts. Examples dealing with the Redeemer follow:

1. "I am Jesus Christ the Son of God. I created the heavens and the earth, and all things that in them are" (3 Ne. 9:15).

These words, spoken in America, give a greatly expanded role for the Savior than is usually accorded Him. John 1:1–14 supports this idea, but most Christians interpret this verse differently.

2. "I am he that gave the law, and I am he who covenanted with my people Israel" (3 Ne. 15:5).

The Savior made it clear that He was the God of the Old Testament people. Biblical prophets, not mentioned in the Old Testament—Zenock, Neum, and Zenos—also prophesied that the God of Abraham, Isaac and Jacob is Jesus Christ (1 Ne. 19:10).

3. "The Spirit of Christ is given to every man, that he may know good from evil" (Moroni 7:16).

That every human upon the earth is endowed with the Spirit of Christ is a unique Book of Mormon concept. Latter-day Saints believe this spirit is similar to what the secular world calls a conscience.

4. Christ in America declared, "Ye are they of whom I said: Other sheep I have which are not of this fold; them also I must bring, and they shall hear my voice" (3 Ne. 15:21).

The Savior was quoting His own words, given earlier in the Holy Land (See John 10:16). Commentators of the New Testament are not sure what this verse means. They usually assume that Christ was speaking

of a future visit He would make to the non-Jews in
their area. However, earlier the Lord had made it clear:
"I am not sent but unto the lost sheep of the house of
Israel" (Matt. 15:24). Also in the Book of Mormon,
Jesus said, "I have other sheep, which are not of this
land (America), neither of the land of Jerusalem"
whom He would yet visit (3 Nephi 16:1).

5. Christ will suffer the crucifixion "that the resurrection might pass upon all men" (2 Ne. 9:22).

Many in Christianity believe that Christ's ordeal
applies only to Christians. However, this and other
Book of Mormon verses give a universal view of
Christ's Atonement. It brings resurrection for all
humanity regardless of belief or performance.

6. "Where there is no law given there is no punishment" (2 Ne. 9:25).

Jacob continued the verse: "And where there is
no punishment there is no condemnation; and where
there is no condemnation the mercies of the Holy
One of Israel have claim upon them, because of the
atonement; for they are delivered by the power of
him" (2 Ne. 9:25). The Book of Mormon mercifully
teaches that ignorance of the law *is* an excuse. Those
who do not know they have committed a sin will not
be punished for it.

7. "Little children need no repentance, neither baptism . . . but little children are alive in Christ" (Moroni 8:11–12).

Using the same logic as in point six, there should be no need for little children to be baptized. The Bible is silent on this issue. The Book of Mormon leaves no doubt and condemns this practice.

8. When baptizing, Christ taught, "Immerse them in the water, and come forth again out of the water" (3 Ne. 11:26; see also Mosiah 18:14).

The Bible makes a reasonable case for immersion as the correct form of baptism. However, the Book of Mormon leaves no doubt. John said Jesus was baptized in the river Jordan "because there was much water there" (John 3:23; See also Matt. 3:16; Acts 8:38; Romans 6:4).

9. Christ was "baptized by water, to fulfil all righteousness . . . and witnesseth unto the Father that he would be obedient unto him in keeping his commandments" (2 Ne. 31:5–7).

Nephi stated that Christ's baptism was to show humility and to set an example to His people, that all must be baptized. The verse also shows that if Christ had to be baptized and be obedient to His Father, so must His followers. The Bible is not clear on this information.

10. In the Book of Mormon, baptisms were done before the Savior was born (Mosiah 18:14).

Many Christians were shocked when the Dead Sea Scrolls spoke of baptisms in Old Testament times. Most people had believed this ordinance was first performed in the days of the Savior's mortal ministry. Critics thought the fact that there were baptisms in the Book of Mormon before Christ came was an anachronism. However, with today's new information, such as found in the Dead Sea Scrolls, this is no longer an issue.

11. The Lord "denieth none that come unto him, black and white . . . and all are alike unto God, both Jew and Gentile" (2 Ne. 26:33).

The closest the Bible comes to dealing with race is the parable of the good Samaritan. In the Book of Mormon, we again see the universal role of the Savior.

12. Christ "will suffer temptations, and pain . . . even more than man can suffer . . . for behold, blood cometh from every pore" (Mosiah 3:7).

The New Testament account states, "His sweat was as it were great drops of blood falling down to the ground" (Luke 22:44). Some biblical commentaries state that in the darkness of night in Gethsemane the drops of sweat were figurative—they only looked like blood because it was dark. The Book of Mormon says the drops were literally blood, making Christ's ordeal even more hard to grasp.

13. The sacrament of the Lord's supper "is in remembrance" of Christ's suffering (3 Ne. 18:7, 11).

The Bible uses the expressions, "take, eat: this is my body" and "this is my blood" (Matt. 26:26, 27; Mark 14:22–24). Thus, the doctrine of transubstantiation (the literal partaking of Christ's flesh and blood), and the modified doctrine of consubstantiation, became part of some versions of Christianity. The Book of Mormon and some passages of the Bible make it clear that partaking of the sacrament is symbolic and not literal.

14. The exact words of Christ's sacramental prayers are preserved (Moroni 4 and 5).

These prayers are not found in the Bible as we have it today.

15. Participation in holy communion is prescribed (3 Ne. 18:28–30).

The Book of Mormon states that the sacrament in remembrance of the Lord's suffering should only be taken worthily. Today in some versions of Christianity, it is taken to receive forgiveness of sins. In some churches, part of the sacrament is not administered to the lay members of the congregation.

16. Jesus' opponent was an angel who "had fallen from heaven . . . became a devil . . . sought also the misery of all mankind . . . [and] is the father of all lies" (2 Ne. 2:17–18).

Although some Christians believe in a literal devil, many believe references to Satan are only figurative. The Bible only occasionally speaks of the devil. The Book of Mormon gives much information about his reality, deceptive methods, and how to guard against him.

17. "O the wisdom of God, his mercy and grace! For behold, if the flesh should rise no more our spirits must become subject to . . . the devil" (2 Ne. 9:8).

This unique Book of Mormon idea adds further clarity and appreciation for our Lord and Savior Jesus Christ. It shows the absolute necessity of His Atonement in thwarting Satan's evil purposes.

18. Jesus said, "I will judge the world, every man according to their works" (2 Ne. 29:11–12).

Our eternal judge will be Jesus Christ, not Peter, as many believe. The Book of Mormon also makes it clear in this verse that God will judge us according to that which is found in scripture.

19. Christ said, "I shall speak unto the Jews and they shall write it [Bible]; and I shall speak unto the Nephites and they shall write it [Book of Mormon];

and I shall also speak to the other tribes of the house of Israel, which I have led away, and they shall write it; and I shall also speak unto all nations of the earth and they shall write it" (2 Ne. 29:12).

Latter-day Saints expect the writings of the other lost tribes of Israel concerning Christ to come forth someday, just as the Book of Mormon came as a record of the tribe of Joseph and some Jews. This Book of Mormon verse states there are more writings of Jesus still to come forth, and it underscores that Jesus is the God of all the inhabitants of the earth, though they do not realize it.

20. Christ "shall go forth suffering pains and afflictions and temptations of every kind . . . and he will take upon him death . . . that he may know according to the flesh how to succor his people according to their infirmities" (Alma 7:11–12).

Only the Book of Mormon gives this as one purpose for Christ's great suffering. His experience would enable Him to nourish and judge humans with experience and compassion.

21. The Savior "himself atoneth for the sins of the world, to bring about the plan of mercy, to appease the demands of justice" (Alma 42:15).

Alma added: "Do ye suppose that mercy can rob justice? I say unto you, Nay; not one whit. If so, God;

would cease to be God"(Alma 42:25). The Lord Himself obeys laws we learn from the Book of Mormon. Christ fulfilled the law of justice by being "crucified and slain . . . having broken the bands of death, taken upon himself their iniquity and their transgressions, having redeemed them, and satisfied the demands of justice" (Mosiah 15:7–9).

22. "O how great the plan of our God!" (2 Ne. 9:13).

The word "plan" appears 42 times in the Book of Mormon, but never in the Bible. Most Christians consider the Fall a shameful sin. The Bible never refers to the Fall of Adam and Eve and the Atonement of Christ as part of a plan. By contrast, the Book of Mormon uses such expressions as "the eternal plan of deliverance" (2 Ne. 11:5), "the plan of redemption," (Alma 12:25), "the plan of salvation" (Jarom 1:2), and "the great plan of happiness" (Alma 42:8). What comfort and peace come to the soul by knowing of Christ's plan for humankind.

23. "Adam fell that men might be; and men are, that they might have joy" (2 Ne. 2:25).

From this verse we learn that joy is desirable in life. These verses explain that without the Fall, Adam and Eve would have no "joy, for they knew no misery; doing no good, for they knew no sin" (2 Ne.

2:23). Thus, for joy to exist, sorrow and suffering must be possibilities.

24. Because of the Atonement men are "free forever, knowing good from evil" (2 Ne. 2:26).

The Book of Mormon makes it clear that real freedom comes only through the Atonement of Jesus Christ and knowing good from evil. The Bible complements this message with Paul's statement, "Where the spirit of the Lord is, there is liberty" (2 Cor. 3:17).

25. "It is by grace that we are saved, after all we can do" (2 Ne. 25:23).

Many Christians believe that the grace of Christ alone will save them. Reading the Bible, one certainly should realize that grace is necessary for salvation. Reading the same Bible, one finds that works are also needed. The logical conclusion is that both are necessary. We see this succinctly in the Book of Mormon verse above.

26. Inasmuch as Christ died for mankind, humans are free "to act for themselves and not be acted upon, save it be by the punishment of the law . . . according to the commandments which God hath given" (2 Ne. 2:26).

We gain great insight as to the importance and necessity of each person's personal responsibility.

27. Jesus said in the last days, if a church is "called in my name then it is my church, if it so be that they are built upon my gospel" (3 Ne. 27:5–8).

The Church of Jesus Christ of Latter-day Saints is one of the few churches that bears the Savior's name and title. Calling a church by Christ's name does not make it His Church unless it also teaches correct principles and has the proper authority. In the New Testament it does say, "The churches of Christ salute you," suggesting that early members of Christ's church referred to themselves by that title (Rom. 16:16). However, Paul's verse is open to interpretation. The word "Christ" is one of the many titles for "Jesus," which is the Savior's actual name. The Book of Mormon makes it perfectly clear that Jesus wants His Church to bear His name and title.

Further readings: Hickenbotham (1995), 191–193; Scharffs (1989), 52–56.

3.2. Does the Book of Mormon have other doctrines that are unique or clarify the Bible?

1. Christians "must repent and be born again" (Alma 5:49).

Nowhere does the Bible speak of being "born again" as an instant saving event that a person experiences in this life, as some Christians are taught. The Bible, in John 3:5, correctly speaks of being "born again" as baptism and receiving the Spirit (Holy Ghost). The Book of Mormon articulates these precise words and also declares that repentance is a prerequisite to being born again.

2. The first four principles and ordinances of the gospel are presented as a unit. (Moroni 8:25–26).

In the Bible we find faith in the Lord Jesus Christ, repentance, baptism and the gift of the Holy Ghost mentioned. Only the Book of Mormon puts these basics in a logical sequence.

3. Followers of Christ must "always retain a remission of your sins" (Mosiah 4:12).

Again we see that salvation is not an event as some Christians maintain, but an ongoing process. The Bible teaches that believers should cease to sin and uses the expression "gaining a remission of sin" seven times. However, only the Book of Mormon uses the expression, "*retain* a remission of your sins" (emphasis added). As an LDS apostle, Neal A. Maxwell stated, "There are no instant Christians, only constant Christians."

4. "The Lord esteemeth all flesh in one; he that is righteous is favored of God" (1 Ne. 17:35).

The Book of Mormon brings new insight to what it means to be a "chosen people" of God. Unfortunately, nationality, race, religion, or wealth often define the phrase "chosen people." Interpreted this way, "chosen people" is a dangerous notion that often leads to hate and even war. History has plenty of such examples. Hitler told Germans they were the Master Race. Shintoism, the state religion of Japan, taught a similar idea, but the emperor renounced it after World War II. The Book of Mormon gives a new dimension to the term. It teaches that the "chosen person" in God's eyes is one who chooses to obey God's commandments, chooses to have charity, chooses to be kind, and chooses to be virtuous.

5. Experimenting with faith is like planting and cultivating a seed (Alma 32:27–43).

There is no greater discourse on how to attain faith and make it grow in all scripture or perhaps in all literature than in the Book of Mormon. Alma explains that the seed grows if nourished. In the same manner, if we plant the seed of faith in our hearts and nourish it, we will discover whether it is true or blind faith. Only the Book of Mormon uses the word *experiment* four times as a sure way to develop faith. Paul also gives a masterful discourse on faith in Hebrews, chapter 11. The two discourses are different and complement each other.

6. Sinners will have punishment "as a lake of fire and brimstone" (Mosiah 3:27).

The Bible calls hell "a lake of fire and brimstone." Should this be interpreted literally or metaphorically? Christians generally accept it literally, but as the quoted verse shows, the Book of Mormon uses the phrase symbolically, making God's punishment more compassionate.

7. "As oft as they repented and sought forgiveness, with real intent, they were forgiven" (Moroni 6:8).

Some make a mockery of repentance, falling into a continuous cycle of sin and repentance. Others say that if you sin again, it was not real repentance, and that you can only really repent once. The Book of Mormon makes allowance for human frailty. It is comforting to know that when one slips after repenting, the door to repentance remains open if a person has *sincere* intentions to change.

8. If Adam and Eve had not transgressed, they "would have remained forever in the Garden of Eden" (2 Ne. 2:22).

It was part of God's plan to allow Adam and Eve to choose mortality on behalf of all of us. However, the Lord did not want to force the mortal experience upon His children. Thus, He gave our first earthly parents two opposing commandments. The Book of Mormon teaches that keeping the second commandment (not eating the forbidden fruit) would have guaranteed a blissful life in the garden forever, but that life would have been without challenges and personal growth. Breaking the lesser commandment allowed Adam and Eve to keep the higher first commandment leading to mortality with all the pain and suffering it would entail. However, it also allowed opportunities for experiences, development, families, and joy that could only flourish in a state of opposition. Thus Latter-day Saints do not look upon the Fall as a tragic evil, but a step planned by God to provide an enriching human experience.

9. After the Fall, Adam and Eve understood "good from evil" (Alma 12:31).

In Genesis the phrase is "to know good *and* evil," which is a significant difference (Gen. 3:22; emphasis added). Perhaps the expression, "We are born to sin," has its roots in the Genesis passage. The Book of Mormon teaches that the purpose of the life experience is to learn the difference between good and evil and to do good. I have found one other translation that agrees with the Book of Mormon. We can learn from our mistakes. Nevertheless, we are better off when we can learn by observing the consequences of sin rather than experiencing the consequences ourselves. Sinners run the risk of being addicted, harmed, or even destroyed by sin.

10. "Adam fell that man might be; and men are, that they might have joy" (2 Ne. 2:25).

From the Book of Mormon we learn that joy is a desirable goal in life. The Book of Mormon is also clear that without the Fall, Adam and Eve would not have had "joy, for they knew no misery, doing no good, for they knew no sin" (2 Ne. 2:23). Thus, for joy to exist, sorrow and suffering must also be present.

11. We must have "an opposition in all things . . . [or] righteousness could not be brought to pass, neither wickedness, neither holiness nor misery, neither good nor bad" (2 Ne. 2:11).

The Book of Mormon makes a significant contribution, helping us understand why God created a world where evil exists. By overcoming wickedness, misery, and evil we develop character. This also sheds light on the philosophical dilemma created by the wrong interpretation of the omnipotence of God. Some incorrectly believe this means God can do anything whatsoever. Thus, many find it hard to believe that an all-powerful, perfect God would create a world with so much evil and suffering. The Book of Mormon explains that a world that has suffering and pain is necessary for goodness to operate, which allows for personal growth and joy.

12. Without the Fall, Adam and Eve "would have had no children" (2 Ne. 2:23).

The Bible states that God's first commandment given to Adam and Eve was to "multiply and replenish the earth" (Gen. 1:28). The second commandment was to not eat the forbidden fruit (See Gen. 2:17). The Bible does not mention that breaking this second commandment enabled the first mortal parents of the human race to have children. This unique contribution of the Book of Mormon makes clear the necessity of transgressing the second commandment to bring about the mortal experience God wanted His children to have. It also enables humans to become co-creators with God in bringing about mortal life for His other spirit children.

13. The Lord said, "I give unto men weakness that they may be humble" (Ether 12:27).

The Book of Mormon adds insight as to why life has its problems. The verse continues: "And my grace is sufficient for all men that humble themselves before me; for if they humble themselves before me, and have faith in me, then will I make weak things become strong." As we achieve success and prosperity, we tend to become proud and arrogant, qualities detrimental to interpersonal relationships. God wants us to overcome pride and have enough humility to rely on Him, thereby gaining real strength. (See also Ether 12:37.)

14. Life "is a state of probation" and a time to repent (2 Ne. 2:21).

"Probation" appears nine times in the Book of Mormon, never in the Bible. Therefore, we gain another insight into dealing with the purpose of life. Life is a time to learn the difference between good and evil, and a time to develop personal character to shun evil and do good.

15. Death comes to all "to fulfil the merciful plan of the great Creator" (2 Ne. 9:6).

The sting of death fades somewhat knowing that death is part of God's plan. Jacob goes on to explain the need for the Savior and the resurrection which He achieved for all people: "O how great the goodness of our God, who prepareth a way for our escape from the grasp of that awful monster; yea, that monster, death and hell" (2 Ne. 9:10).

16. "Ye shall never taste of death . . . but . . . shall be changed in the twinkling of an eye from mortality to immortality" (3 Ne. 28:7–8).

The New Testament speaks of the apostle John never tasting of death, and many have wondered what this means (John 21:22–24). The Book of Mormon explains that John was translated and will dwell on the earth until the Second Coming of Christ. The Book of Mormon also says the same is true of three Nephite disciples and Moses. The account of the death of Moses in Deuteronomy 34:5–8 is also vague.

17. If God were to disobey law, "God would cease to be God" (Alma 42:25).

It is comforting to know that God always obeys eternal laws. Thus, the Lord Himself obeys rules as He expects of us.

18. "I also beheld that the tree of life was a representation of the love of God" (1 Ne. 11:25).

The tree of life is mentioned several times in the Bible, beginning with Adam and Eve. It is also found in ancient art and carvings throughout the world, including Central America, where many Latter-day Saints believe the Book of Mormon story took place. Both Lehi and Nephi had visions of the tree of life and gave a very detailed description of this important symbol. The Book of Mormon equates the act of partaking of the tree's fruit with mortals experiencing God's love.

19. The Lord said, "I will liken thee, O house of Israel, like unto a tame olive-tree" (Jacob 5:3).

A few verses in Romans 11 contain a reference to an allegory about olive trees. However, Jacob 5 is the longest chapter in the Book of Mormon, consisting of seven and one-half pages. The allegory was first written by Zenos, a prophet from Old Testament times who is not found in the Bible. The account of Jacob in the Book of Mormon must have been taken from the brass plates that were retrieved from Laban at the time Lehi sent his sons back to Jerusalem to obtain the records, before their departure to America. The plates were important to the Nephites because it was their only scriptural link to Jerusalem. They were commanded by God to flee Jerusalem just prior to the destruction of that city, its temple, and the Babylonian captivity of the surviving Jews.

It is impossible to conceive how Joseph Smith or anyone in the United States could have known the importance and intricacies of Middle Eastern olive tree horticulture. These evergreen trees are abundant in the Middle East, where they grow so well and are essential to the existence of the inhabitants where Zenos lived. Olive oil was used in lamps, heating, cooking, a condiment for salads, bread and meat, anointing, temple rituals, and medication. No olive trees existed anywhere near Joseph Smith's New England environment. In this single chapter of the Book of Mormon we find many detailed practices and procedures that almost no one in the United States in the early 1800s would have known, especially an unlearned Joseph Smith.

The allegory is a story of mankind's destiny, outlining the history of the world, and stresses that performance is more important than lineage and those who have the gospel must share it with others. It goes on to demonstrate God's infinite love for all His children, and that He strives to bless them again and again.

Further Reading: Ricks and Welch (1994).

20. Jesus said, "Search these [scriptures] diligently; for great are the words of Isaiah" (3 Ne. 23:1).

Five percent of the Book of Mormon is made up of quotations from Isaiah. Yet this is not odd, because Jewish tradition considers him the greatest prophet between Samuel and the end of the Old Testament. Book of Mormon people, especially the Savior and Nephi, loved Isaiah, who lived less than a century before Lehi's family fled Jerusalem for America. More quotes from Isaiah are found in the Bible and the Dead Sea Scrolls, as well as in the Book of Mormon, than any other biblical prophet. Jesus, Peter, Paul and John quote 42 Isaiah verses in the Bible. Of the 433 Isaiah verses in the Book of Mormon, 234 are different from the Bible and many verses say something concerning the Savior.

21. "Blessed are the poor in spirit who come unto me," Christ taught in America (3 Ne. 12:3).

In His Sermon on the Mount by the Sea of Galilee, Jesus taught, "Blessed are the poor in spirit; for theirs is the kingdom of heaven" (Matt 5:3).

Biblical scholars have wondered how someone "poor in spirit" merits the kingdom of heaven. To make sense, some say this means humility. The Book of Mormon version clarifies: someone who turns to Christ will be entitled to the reward.

22. "Whosoever is angry with his brother shall be in danger of his judgment" (3 Ne, 12:22).

King James reads: "Whosoever is angry with his brother without a cause . . . ." (Matt. 5:22). It seems like a cause can always be found to be angry with someone. The verse in the Book of Mormon simply says: "Whosoever is angry with his brother . . ." without qualification (3 Ne. 12:22). The contribution of the Book of Mormon is that anger is not the way to solve problems.

Further Reading: Welch (1990).

23. "My soul hungered . . . and I cried unto [God] in mighty prayer" (Enos 1:4; 2 Ne. 4:24).

Both the Bible and Book of Mormon teach the importance of prayer. The Book of Mormon adds some specific insights. We learn that the evil spirit (Satan) "teacheth a man not to pray" (2 Ne. 32:8). We also read that prayer is not optional in our lives if we want to obey God, and it is a sin not to pray (See Ether 2:14–15). We also discover that God might postpone His judgements on the wicked world in response to prayer (See Alma 10:22–23). We also learn specific reasons to pray: for humility, to gain charity, for our crops and flocks, for all in our household, for all around us, and for power to resist the devil and our enemies (See Alma 34:19–29).

24. "This high priesthood . . . being without beginning of days or end of years" (Alma 13:7).

In the book of Hebrews it states that Melchizedek, king of Salem was "without father, without mother . . . having neither beginning of days, nor end of life" (Heb. 7:1–3). Thus, some have called him the most mysterious man in the Bible. The Book of Mormon clarifies the biblical translation we have today by making it clear that it is the Melchizedek Priesthood, not Melchizedek, that is without beginning or end.

3.3. What insights do we find in the Book of Mormon on today's moral issues?

1. "To be learned is good if they hearken unto the counsels of God" (2 Ne. 9:29).

Finding a more succinct statement on the perspective God has concerning the relationship between education and religion would be difficult. The Lord loves faithful scholars, but at least one study shows that the more education some achieve, the less religious they become. With Latter-day Saints, the study shows that more education means more commitment to the Church. (*Church News*, 16 October 1983, 3; see Scharffs (1989), 41).

2. "Before ye seek for riches, seek ye for the kingdom of God" (Jacob 2:18–19).

In the Bible and Book of Mormon are many verses that caution against wealth. Some in society hold poverty as the ideal; others consider wealth as the sign of success. Both views are extreme and wrong. Jacob's words do not condemn wealth, but state that a person's priorities must be righteousness and generosity. Jacob also makes it clear that the reward for virtue is not automatically wealth. The above quotation continues, "And after ye have obtained a hope in Christ ye shall obtain riches, if ye seek them; and ye will seek them for the intent to do good."

3. "They were fighting for their homes and their liberties, their wives and their children" (Alma 43:45).

In society there are doves and hawks when it comes to war. The Book of Mormon condemns war, but is specific about when righteous defensive action is warranted. Once, the Book of Mormon Nephites wanted to attack their enemies before their enemies had a chance to attack them. Their prophet warned against such a preemptive strike: "The Lord forbid;

for if we should go up against them the Lord would deliver us into their hands; therefore we will prepare ourselves . . . and wait till they shall come against us" (3 Ne. 3:20–21).

4. "It is not expedient [to have] . . . kings to rule over you" (Mosiah 29:16).

Mosiah also said if it were always possible to have good kings it would be proper for kings to rule over their people. However, since it was hard to remove bad kings, it would be better to choose "by the voice of the people, judges, that they may be judged according to the laws which have been given you by . . . the hand of the Lord" (Mosiah 29:25). The Book of Mormon has many insights on good government. However, one main message is that no government will work if the leaders and people are wicked.

5. Fornication is "most abominable above all sins save it be the shedding of innocent blood or denying the Holy Ghost" (Alma 39:5).

The Bible clearly teaches against every kind of sexual impurity. The Book of Mormon contribution is that sexual sin is next to murder in seriousness. Since the prophet Alma spoke these words to his single wayward son Corianton, this iniquity is in the same category as adultery for married people. Alma made it clear that his son could repent of this evil action, which Corianton did. He spent years of faithful service doing God's work. Both the Bible and the Book of Mormon rank sinning against the Holy Ghost as the unpardonable sin (Matt. 12:31).

6. "When they saw your conduct they would not believe in my words" (Alma 39:11).

The power of example, good or bad, is inferred throughout the Bible, but these words of Alma to his son in the previous incident make it most clear. Years of Alma's preaching to the people to repent were hindered by his son's actions. To his credit, Corianton spent much effort trying to undo the damage he had done.

7. "See that ye bridle all your passions, that ye may be filled with love" (Alma 38:12).

Today, immorality is portrayed in attractive ways almost nonstop by the media and in literature. We hear few who proclaim the ideal of chastity. Many mistake lust for love and get trapped in horrible consequences: disease, unwanted children, and a loss of the love they were seeking. Some try to deny all passions; others let lust rule their lives. In this verse, Alma allows for the appropriate use of our urges and desires. In the same verse, he teaches us to refrain from idleness in order to help curb inappropriate feelings. Controlling our passions would also help eliminate hate, envy, selfishness, anger, and other vices. This verse in the Book of Mormon gives us one of the greatest definitions of true love.

CHAPTER FOUR
Book of Mormon Evidences

4.1. Do Latter-day Saints claim that the Book of Mormon is an ancient history of the Americas?

The LDS Church does not maintain that the Book of Mormon is an account of all the pre-Columbian people who resided in the Americas. It covers groups confined to a radius of a few hundred miles. Other groups who arrived in ships or crossed the Bering Strait certainly came to the Western Hemisphere. Several years after the families of Lehi and Ishmael arrived, Father Lehi died. Afterward, there was a split in the group. Some of the family, who followed the son Nephi, departed from the followers of son Laman. "I, Nephi, did take my family, and also Zoram and his family, and Sam, mine elder brother and his family, and Jacob and Joseph, my younger brethren, and also my sisters, and all those who would go with me" (2 Ne. 5:6).

Offshoot groups and descendants of Book of Mormon people were undoubtedly assimilated with other societies or formed separate communities elsewhere in the Western Hemisphere. Their history is not recorded in the Book of Mormon. A mystery (seldom discussed) is what happened to the main group of Book of Mormon Nephites, who disappeared two or three hundred years after their first arrival in the Western Hemisphere. Under the first King Mosiah, a minority of the people in the land of Nephi left to get away from wicked conditions (Omni 1:12–14). These Nephites joined up with a much larger group of Jews called Mulekites, living in Zarahemla. The Mulekites, led by one of the sons of King Zedekiah, had fled Jerusalem (soon after the Lehi group left), at the time Babylonians ravaged the city. These Mulekites had not kept any records over the centuries. With the arrival of the Nephites, many of them certainly had wandered away before and after they settled Zarahemla.

After many years, some of the Nephites living in Zarahemla, led by Zeniff, returned to the land of Nephi only to find it devoid of all Nephites who had lived there before. The Book of Mormon gives no account of what happened to them. Perhaps they were driven away by the Lamanites who now controlled the land. Another dispersion of Book of Mormon people happened around 50 B.C. At this time, groups of Book of Mormon people sailed away in ships built by Hagoth, to go to northern lands, and some were never heard from again (Alma 63:7–8).

Further Reading: Welch (1992), 1–34.

4.2. Isn't it unlikely that a small ship could cross the ocean during pre-Columbian times?

This was the thinking in Joseph Smith's day, but today there are many records of pre-Columbian ocean crossings to the New World. John L. Sorenson and Martin H. Raish have published a two-volume work that contains hundreds of entries supporting such transocean voyages. In recent years, the journeys of Norwegian explorer Thor Heyerdahl proved that journeys of small ocean craft were possible across the Pacific Ocean.

Further Readings: Griffith (1993), 44; Sorenson and Raish (1990).

4.3. Have other metal plates been found that contain ancient writings?

Researchers have discovered many writings on plates (including gold) from antiquity since the time of Joseph Smith, giving credence to the Book of Mormon. Metal plates of gold and silver inscribed during the reign of Darius I of Persia (518–515 B.C.) have been found in that land. They were sealed in a box of stone, as were the Book of Mormon plates.

Further Readings: Nibley (1964); Sorenson (1992).

4.4. Isn't there a great deal of archaeological proof for the Bible and none for the Book of Mormon?

Archaeological evidence exists for both the Bible and the Book of Mormon, but proof does not. The science of archaeology deals with material remains of ancient civilizations. Archaeologist Michael Coe, formerly of the Smithsonian Institute and now head of the archaeology department at Yale University, stated: "Not even the best and most advanced research has established on purely archaeological grounds the historical details of the Bible, for instance the existence of Jesus Christ" *(Dialogue: A Journal of Mormon Thought*, Summer 1973, 41–46).

4.5. What external evidence is there to support the validity of the Book of Mormon?

External evidence is not necessary to validate the Book of Mormon. The Book of Mormon speaks for itself. Its truth is made manifest through study, pondering, and prayer. Nevertheless, the Lord has encouraged us to "seek learning, even by study and also by faith" (D&C 88:118). Latter-day Saints like to point out evidence for the Book of Mormon when it comes forth in the same manner as other Christians like to see verification for the Bible. The LDS Church does not claim to prove the book by external evidence. God has given ample evidence by restoring the book. The power of the Book of Mormon lies in its teachings. However, linguistic, grammatical, literary, geographical, and cultural studies, as well as archaeology, give a great deal of evidence for the authenticity of the Book of Mormon. Some examples follow.

1. Worship of a white god in Mesoamerica.

For dark-skinned people to worship a white god seems abnormal. Quetzalcoatl, meaning "feathered serpent", became the symbol for the white god of the Mayans. This deity opposed human sacrifice and taught definite ways of life. He is also associated with death and resurrection. Quetzalcoatl represents a god who was the creator of all things, was born of a virgin, and performed miracles. He was a universal god and promised to return.

Quetzal is a bird with a beautiful colorful feathered plume found in Mesoamerica. Almost extinct, it is rarely seen today, but is still the national bird in Guatemala. Some believe that Coatl, the serpent part of the symbol, has biblical origin. Moses represented Jesus Christ to the children of Israel in the wilderness when he raised a serpent on a pole as a symbol of the Savior's coming Atonement (Num. 21:8; 1 Ne. 17:41; Alma 33:18-22). The Book of Mormon people knew the "Serpent/Savior" story from the Old Testament brass plates they brought out of Jerusalem. Some Latter-day Saints feel that since Christ descended out of the heavens, feathers of the Quetzal bird eventually became part of the motif. This symbol, used very early in Mesoamerica, was revived later when the wicked survivors of the Book of Mormon became pagan. Then their form of worship and Quetzalcoatl became a substitute for the earlier appearance of Jesus Christ.

2. Steel, iron, cement, wheels, silk, linen, horses, elephants, barleys, highways, metal plates, etc.

For nearly a century after Joseph Smith published the Book of Mormon, such things were considered anachronisms. Today, evidence of such items has been found, mostly by non-LDS scholars. For example, the Book of Mormon mentions "barley" (Welch, 1992, 130). Scholars made this discovery in Mesoamerica in recent years. Horses, believed to have been first introduced by the Spaniards, were mentioned in the Book of Mormon. New findings show that accounts of horses in Book of Mormon times should not be considered "erroneous or unhistorical" (Welch 1992, 98–100).

3. Dark and light-skinned people existed in Mesoamerica.

Murals showing light- and dark-skinned people have been found at Bonampak in the southern Mexican state of Chiapas. The art shows darker people as masters, and light-skinned people apparently as slaves.

Perhaps this depicts the Book of Mormon practice of Lamanites enslaving Nephites (Sorenson, 1985, 82).

4. The Tree of Life Story

C. Wilfred Griggs, of Brigham Young University, has pointed out the striking similarity between the Book of Mormon Tree of Life story with other sixth and seventh-century B.C. texts found in burial sites in the Mediterranean area. Dr. Griggs found these writings and noted the Near Eastern, or more particularly Egyptian, origin of the texts. He then compared Lehi's dream with these ancient sources. He concluded that "the Book of Mormon account is similar both to the writings on metal tablets and to the related Egyptian literature" (Reynolds (1982), 75).

In 1951, M. Wells Jakeman, then chair of the BYU archaeology department, claimed a stone (Stela No. 5) in Izapa, Mexico, depicted Lehi's vision of the tree of life in the Book of Mormon (1 Ne. 8; Jakeman, 1958). Some LDS scholars, associated with F.A.R.M.S especially, today strongly feel Dr. Jakeman's interpretation is incorrect.

5. The ancient literary technique known as chiasmus.

Many forms of parallelism are in the Bible and Book of Mormon. One form, chiasmus, is a rhetorical device sometimes used in the Bible and in other ancient literature, including histories of the Mayan. It is reverse parallelism. A simple parallelism reads as follows:

"A soft answer turneth away wrath:
But grievous words stir up anger" (Prov. 15:1)

A chiasmus in its simplest form:
"[The] first shall be last and
the last shall be first" (Matt. 19:30).

One of many examples from the Book of Mormon:

A. Whosoever shall not take upon him the name of Christ

B. must be called by some other name;

C. therefore, he findeth himself on the left hand of God.

D. And I would that ye should remember also, that this is the name . . .

E. that never should be blotted out [of your hearts.]

F. except it be through transgression;

F. therefore, take heed that ye do not transgress,

E. that the name be not blotted out of your hearts . . .

D. I would that ye should remember to retain

the name . . .

C. that ye are not found on the left hand of God,

B. but that ye hear and know the voice by which ye shall be called,

A. and also, the name by which he shall call you. (Mosiah 5:10–12)

Chiasmus was unnoticed by modern Western Civilization until the middle of the nineteenth century, after Joseph Smith's time. Dr. John W. Welch was the first to notice many examples of chiasmus in the Book of Mormon. This is remarkable evidence of the ancient origin of the Book of Mormon (Reynolds, 1982, 34).

Further Readings: Reynolds (1997), 99–224; Welch (1992), 36, 152–53, 230–32, 233–35.

6. The Babylonians did not kill King Zedekiah's son, Mulek.

According to the Bible, the Babylonian troops captured the last King of Judah, Zedekiah, and forced him to watch the execution of his sons. They also put out his eyes, and took him captive to Babylon (2 Kings 25:4–7). According to the Book of Mormon, however, one son named Mulek escaped and came to America with a group of Jews. Some biblical scholars now feel they have identified a son of Zedekiah whom the Babylonians did not kill. They also feel his abbreviated name could well be Mulek. Researcher Robert F. Smith quotes a prominent non-Mormon ancient Near Eastern specialist: "If Joseph Smith came up with that one he did [very well]" (Welch 1992, 142–144).

7. Forty-day Literature.

Dr. Hugh B. Nibley compared the account of Christ's ministry in America found in 3 Nephi with the "Forty-day Literature" and discovered striking parallels and similarities. The Forty-Day Literature consists of non-biblical Christian writings that deal with Christ's teachings to His disciples during the forty days after His resurrection. The material speaks of Book of Mormon themes such as forthcoming apostasy. It makes clear Christ's ministry extended beyond the Holy Land, with the Savior appearing in other parts of the world. These writings emphasize Christ sending out missionaries to preach His message and describe Christ's physical resurrection and eating the emblems of the sacrament. (A similarity of sacrament prayers was found with those in the Book of Mormon.) The Forty-day Literature also speaks of additional higher teachings of Christ that were too sacred to reveal. They reaffirmed the need for baptism and Christ's visits to the spirit prison to organize His Church. Much of the Forty-day literature was found along the Nile in Egypt in a community called Nag

Hamdi. These writings have shed light on the New Testament as the Dead Sea Scrolls did for the Old Testament. Dr. Nibley made a side-by-side comparison with Book of Mormon passages in his article that appeared in *Book of Mormon Authorship* (Reynolds, 1982, 121–141).

8. The Popol Vuh Mayan history.

The Spaniards destroyed practically all writings of Mesoamerica. The Popol Vuh is a Mesoamerican document by a Quiche Indian written shortly after the Spanish Conquest in 1550. This tribe is a branch of the Mayan in Guatemala. Because of the destruction of the written records, the author relied on oral traditions to recreate the records. The Popol Vuh contains traditions of the creation, the flood, the origin of the Quiche nations, and the genealogy of its kings. It declares first and second migrations from the Middle East, which corresponds to the two major migrations to the Western Hemisphere in the Book of Mormon.

The Popol Vuh also speaks of a white god and white people. These people were monogamous, as were righteous people in the Book of Mormon. The text describes one king who was over the entire land and sub-kings who operated under them, as was the practice by the Book of Mormon Lamanites. This is the most famous Mayan history and they consider it sacred. The Popol Vuh claims that the Mayan beginnings go back to a common ancestor, as do the Bible and Book of Mormon in their accounts of Adam and Eve. The Popol Vuh used the literary technique called chiasmus, as does the Bible and Book of Mormon and many other ancient writings (Reynolds (1997), 432, 438–39, 502). Some Mormon scholars believe this record describes mostly Lamanites before and after Book of Mormon ended.

Further Readings: Allen (1989), 132–33; Hunter and Ferguson (1950).

9. The writings of Ixtlitxochitl

Born of Spanish and Mexican royalty, Fernando de Alva Ixtlixochitl (1578–1650) grew up near Mexico City. His works were first published in English in London in 1848, sixteen years after the Book of Mormon. Since most records were destroyed, he based his history on paintings of his ancestors. Parallels between his writings and the Book of Mormon are uncanny. The first civilization came from the great tower at the time of the confusion of tongues. A white god was born of a virgin who ascended to heaven after teaching His people. Great destruction occurred in the first month of the 34th year (the time when Christ died). Three distinct civilizations predated the coming of the white god. The destruction of the first civilization predated the coming of the white god, as stated in the Book of Mormon. One principal area where the people dwelt was "land of abundance" or Bountiful, as the Nephites called it (Allen (1989), 138–139).

10. Word print analysis of literary style.

Word print analysis is a method of determining an idiosyncratic pattern in the writing of any author. In a way, using this method to analyze literature to determine authorship is similar to the use of finger-prints and DNA in identifying humans. Dr. Wayne A. Larsen and Dr. Alvin C. Rencher conclude that different authors wrote each section of the Book of Mormon. They also found that no Book of Mormon passages resemble the writing of any of the common-ly suggested nineteenth-century authors. "The clear yet previously unnoticed characteristics of the Book of Mormon, discovered by Larsen and Rencher, strongly support Joseph Smith's account of the book's origin" (Reynolds (1982), 158).

Noel B. Reynolds also recently reported that "Applied physicist John L. Hilton and five of his fel-low scientists in the Bay Area (three of them non-LDS) repeated the study using a wholly different and more conservative form of word-printing analysis. Again, they detected different authors, and none cor-responded to the nineteenth-century candidates" (Reynolds (1998), 44).

11. "And it came to pass . . ."

This phrase occurs in the English translation of the Book of Mormon 1,381 times. The Bible uses the expression 613 times. Apparently, the Mayans adopted the phrase. Recently uncovered glyphs of Palenque in Mexico reveal the phrase, "and then it came to pass." Lately, another glyph has been interpreted as "and it shall come to pass." The noted Mayan scholar, Eric Thompson, first observed and recorded these glyphs that followed a pattern on marking dates, which is similar to Book of Mormon usage (See Allen (1998), 32–33). Some ask why the phrase was on the plates so often when space was so limited. The answer: The entire phrase in Hebrew and Egyptian is represented by just one symbol and takes up very little space (Hickenbotham (1995), 223).

12. Pre-exile Classic Hebraisms are more prominent than later biblical Hebrew.

Hebraisms refer to a particular writing style that is peculiar to the Hebrew language. Scholars point out that Old Testament Hebrew, after the Babylonian captivity, changed significantly. Since Book of Mormon people left Jerusalem before the language modification, it is logical that classical Biblical Hebrew expressions are found. Hebrew student Angela M. Crowell, working on her Ph.D at the University of Missouri-Kansas City, was the first to notice this phenomenon. "The phrase *and it came to pass,* the interjection *behold,* and the compound expressions *house of Israel* and *children of Israel* appear more frequently in pre-exile biblical writings than in post-exile books" (*F.A.R.M.S. Insights,* Dec. 1996, 4).

13. Weights and measures in units of one, two, four, seven.

With space on the plates scarce, some wonder why Mormon would take precious room to give an exhaustive, detailed description of Nephite weights and measures (Alma 11:1–20). It is interesting that today in the highlands of Guatemala, in the isolated village of Santiago Atitlan, the same units of weights (1, 2, 4, and 7) are used in the markets. Some have suggested that this could be a bit of evidence for the authenticity of the Book of Mormon.

14. Biblical Jacob saw a "remnant of the coat" of many colors of his son Joseph. (Alma 46:24).

Although not mentioned in the Bible, the Book of Mormon states that Jacob saw a part of the coat had not decayed. However, Muhammed ibn-Ibrahim at-Tha'labi, a Moslem historian, supports the above quoted verse from the book of Alma. The Moslem historian also wrote that a remnant of Joseph's coat became the possession of Father Jacob (see Ludlow (1976), 234).

15. The consistency of the material is remarkable. Similar phrases (and in one case an odd new word) appear from time to time in the Book of Mormon, sometimes hundreds of pages apart, and have been pointed out by Book of Mormon researcher John Welch. He also noted that these phrases were translated by Joseph Smith weeks apart (Welch (1992), 21–23). When Joseph Smith took a break in translating, including starting again the next day, he never asked the scribes to repeat the last lines he had dictated. Translators Martin Harris and Oliver Cowdery became two of the three witnesses to the Book of Mormon. For example: Alma wrote that as Lehi had experienced, he too "saw, God sitting upon his throne, surrounded with numberless concourses of angels, in the attitude of singing and praising their God" (Alma 36:22). Alma had undoubtedly heard and read father Lehi's words often and could therefore quote them and apply them to his situation. However, for any author in the 1800s who never referred to what he had written yesterday or several weeks ago, it would be impossible. Lehi had originally used the exact words earlier, he "thought he saw God sitting upon his throne, surrounded with numberless concourses of angels in the attitude of singing and praising their God" (1 Ne. 1:8).

Now close this page and try quoting these exact twenty-one words. It should be easier for you because you have read them twice in the last minute. Weeks have not gone by since your only exposure to the words, as with Joseph Smith, nor were the words underlined as they are in this text. Dr. Welch makes an interesting observation. If Joseph had asked his scribe, Oliver Cowdery, to go back and read the 21 words from Lehi that he now wanted to repeat, it would have undermined Oliver's confidence in the prophet Joseph Smith (Ibid.).

Early in Book of Mormon history, King Benjamin set forth a five-part legal series prohibiting *murder, plunder, theft, adultery, and any manner of wickedness*. This list first appears in Mosiah 2:13. It again appears several more times including Mosiah 29:36; Alma 23:3; 30:10; Helaman 3:14; and 6:23.

Samuel, a Lamanite prophet on the wall at Zarahemla, spoke of the "coming of Jesus Christ, the Son of God, the Father of heaven and of earth, the Creator of all things from the beginning" (Helaman 14:12). Much earlier King Benjamin recited these exact words which had been given him by an angel (see Mosiah 3:8).

Alma gave a strange name to each of several different weights, the smallest being a "senine." The Savior arrived over a century later and gave his Sermon on the Mount at the temple in Bountiful. Here the Lord used the word "senine" instead of the minuscule "farthing" as He did in the Bible (Matt.

117

5:26; 3 Ne. 12:26). To recall this smallest weight from a long list of names after many pages and many days of translation, would be a remarkable, if not an impossible feat. However, it was a logical change in the sermon by the Savior, who knew that "senine" instead of "farthing" was proper in America. Christ's usage of "farthing" in a Nephite setting would not be comprehended by His listeners.

Some five hundred references to rivers, mountains, forests, lands, and cities are made in the Book of Mormon. Each is referred to once or twice, a few times or very frequently. Although the locations are sometimes mentioned many years and hundreds of pages apart, they fit a consistent pattern. It would be impossible for anyone fabricating the Book of Mormon to keep these locations in mind unless they started with a map in hand.

A study of the remarkable consistencies in the Book of Mormon includes, not only such textual examples, but doctrines, literary styles, teachings, geography, names, places and Hebraisms. The only reasonable explanation is that Joseph, with divine assistance, was working from an actual text. As Book of Mormon scholar Robert Matthews observed: "The complexity of the Book of Mormon is a witness of its historicity" (Matthews, 1966, 64).

Further Readings: Welch (1990), 96–97; Reynolds (1987), 21–38.

4.6. Do the ancient customs of the Middle East coincide with the practices of Lehi's group?

Hugh Nibley has called attention to unusual practices, differing from an American point of view, such as not building fires (this would attract robbers); taking grain and seeds with them (they could not possibly take enough food for such a long journey); naming landmarks along the way after family members (river of Laman). These are all common practices of seasoned desert travelers in that part of the world. Dr. Nibley also points out the interesting way father Lehi admonished his son Lemuel: "O that thou mightest be like unto this valley, firm and steadfast" (1 Ne. 2:10). This is an odd expression for a rural New York boy, Joseph Smith. In America we say, "firm as the mountains." However, to desert travelers, the image of stability is a valley, and this expression is common (Nibley, 1952, 47–91). The Book of Mormon is not a reflection of the early United States, where Joseph Smith lived, but an accurate portrayal of the time and location of when and where the events took place.

4.7. Does the Book of Mormon reflect racist cowboy vs. Indian stories in early U.S. history?

Those who claim Joseph Smith produced the Book of Mormon by borrowing from his environment say the wars reflect the conflicts between cowboys and Indians that were happening in the United States. "The only good Indian is a dead Indian," John Wayne and others often stated in movies depicting early American attitudes toward Native Americans. To suggest that Nephites (white good guys) and Lamanites (dark bad guys) represent this idea is a superficial and completely false understanding of the Book of Mormon.

There was only one race in two thousand years of on-again off-again war among the first group of Book of Mormon people (Jaredites). The second group of settlers, after they divided, consisted of light-skinned Nephites and dark-skinned Lamanites. However, some battles occurred within Nephite groups and among the Lamanite people, independent of each other. The prophet Nephi at the beginning of the Book of Mormon taught, "black and white . . . all are alike unto God" (2 Ne. 26:33). This was certainly *not* a universal attitude in the slavery era of the United States when the Book of Mormon came forth. Jacob, Nephi's brother who succeeded him, warned his people that in some ways the Lamanites were more righteous than they were. He also warned, "revile no more against them because of the darkness of their skins" (Jacob 3:5–9). The racial distinction was not too significant after the Nephites converted thousands of Lamanites, who then became Nephites. Belief in Christ, not skin color, divided Book of

Mormon Nephites and Lamanites. Nephites believed in the Savior, and Lamanites did not.

Unlike United States history, the dark-skinned Lamanites were the victors, and they destroyed the Nephites at the end of the Book of Mormon. The book also speaks of a glorious future and promise for the Lamanites (a remnant of the house of Israel) in the last days, underscoring God's love for all His children, regardless of skin color. There really are few, if any parallels between conflicts in the Book of Mormon and early U.S. history.

Further Reading: Reynolds (1987), 21–38.

4.8. Is it possible that Joseph Smith, or any person or group of people, could have written the Book of Mormon?

Hopefully, chapters three, four, and five of this book show that it would have been impossible. The Book of Mormon structure is complicated, detailed, intricate, and the message is profound and inspiring. Although basically a book giving additional testimony of Jesus Christ and His teachings, the Book of Mormon also has many specifics that are open to scrutiny.

Hugh Nibley quoted Frederich Blass, who gave rules on writing history. "No man on earth can falsify a history of any length without contradicting himself." (Reynolds, 1997, 180–81). Many have the talent to write stories. However, to write ancient history from the great flood (about 2700 B.C.) to A.D. 421, giving great detail, and to claim it as accurate history, is simply impossible.

Those who aided Joseph Smith in the translation state that he had nothing at his disposal except the plates and translation devices. His wife Emma said, "I wrote for Joseph Smith during the work of translation. . . . The larger part of this labor was done [in] my presence and where I could see and know what was being done. . . . During no part of it did Joseph Smith have any [manuscripts] or book of any kind from which to read or dictate except the metallic plates that I knew he had" (Reynolds (1987), 160). Emma also told her son, "Joseph Smith could neither write nor dictate a coherent and well-worded letter, let alone dictate a book like the Book of Mormon. It would have been improbable that a learned man could do this, and for one as unlearned as he was it was simply impossible" (Reynolds (1997), 160).

4.9. Does the LDS Church claim Mesoamerica is the land of the Book of Mormon?

The Church of Jesus Christ of Latter-day Saints takes no position on where Book of Mormon events took place or where sites were located. Most members are primarily concerned with the profound spiritual aspects of the Book of Mormon. This is also my personal quest with emphasis on learning the messages and doctrines of this sacred volume of scripture. However, members of the Church and especially teachers and missionaries should be aware of the studies and new information that pertains to the Book of Mormon as it becomes available.

4.10. How could the warring Nephites and Lamanites be associated with the Mayans since they were such a peaceful civilization?

In recent years, scholars have found that the Mayan civilization had many wars and were extremely violent.

4.11. Why does the Book of Mormon contain so many wars?

By recording armed conflict during a three thousand-year period, the Book of Mormon reflects the sad realities of history. What era of the world has not been plagued with wars? Most of the classics of pre-modern world literature focused on war and God, as did the Old Testament, which parallels much Book of Mormon history.

Perhaps the main reason for the inclusion of war in the Book of Mormon is to warn us of the evils, suffering, and futility of initiating armed conflict. Disobeying God's commandments leads to such bloodshed and carnage. The Book of Mormon proclaimed "the preaching of the word had a great tendency to lead the people to do that which was just—yea, it had had more powerful effect upon the minds of the people than the sword" (Alma 31:5).

Further Readings: EM (1992), 162–166; Reynolds (1997), 524–543.

4.12. What purpose does all the military detail in the Book of Mormon serve?

The fact that the writers were military leaders makes attention to military matters understandable. In any event, so much detail about wars provides evidence for the sacred record.

The military detail further refutes the claim of some critics that Joseph Smith, as author of the Book of Mormon, reflected his early American New England environment. A close study of the military conflicts in the Book of Mormon attests otherwise. William J. Hamblin points out:

> Joseph Smith lived in the age of modern, or technical warfare following the great military transformations of both the sixteenth century and Napoleonic wars. Yet, the Book of Mormon consistently reflects the basic pattern of [warfare] as it was practiced in the Book of Mormon time period. These patterns . . . are not limited to generalities, but also extend to the minutest details of the text (Reynolds (1997), 526).

The author goes on to quote scholars who have found that Book of Mormon warfare fits into the unique Mesoamerican terrain. The lack of any mention of animals during battles (contrary to the Eastern Hemisphere) coincides with what scholars know about Mesoamerican battles. On the other hand, the details of weapons and armor in the Book of Mormon are consistent with ancient practices in other parts of the world at that time. The surrendering of armies when the leader was captured or killed is true in the Book of Mormon as elsewhere during that era. Guerrilla warfare happened in the Book of Mormon, which fits other ancient patterns, as well as a pattern being revived today, called terrorism.

The Book of Mormon use of oaths and customs of surrender is consistent with customs of the Middle East in that day. Tribal loyalty, pre-gunpowder weapons, extensive scouting and spying, pre-battle councils, holy wars, use of banners and military units of tens, fifties, and hundreds are other similarities. Researcher Hamblin concludes: "In many of these topics, the Book of Mormon uniquely reflects its dual heritage of the ancient Near East and Mesoamerica," not the nineteenth-century military methods used in Joseph Smith's day (Ibid.).

Further Readings: Sorenson and Thorne (1991), 242–256; Winward (1995) 48.

4.13. How reliable are the eleven Book of Mormon witnesses?

The Book of Mormon twice prophesied that three witnesses would be shown the plates by an angel, hear the voice of God, and "know of a surety that these things are true" (Ether 5:3–4; 2 Ne. 27:15–20). If Joseph Smith was composing the Book of Mormon, he certainly would not dare make such a prophecy. The chances of that happening seem impossible, unless it really happened. The witnesses had cause to renounce their testimony when they were cut off from the Church. However, they did not because they knew that the Book of Mormon and its divine origins were true.

In some famous recent court trials it would have been extremely vital to the outcome if the prosecution or the defense could have secured only one eyewitness. Only one witness decides some cases and often only by circumstantial evidence. Imagine a court case that has eleven eyewitnesses testifying.

Three of the witnesses—Oliver Cowdery, David Whitmer and Martin Harris—testified of an angel showing them the records and a voice from heaven declaring the plates translated through "the gift and power of God" (Book of Mormon, Introduction). The additional eight witnesses said "[we saw] and did handle with our hands; and we also saw the engravings thereon. . . . And this we bear record with words of soberness . . . for we have seen and hefted, and know of a surety . . . to witness unto the world that which we have seen. And we lie not, God bearing witness of it." All eleven witnesses maintained their original declaration. These witnesses led decent, productive lives, received no monetary gain, and were often ridiculed for their testimonies.

After being excommunicated from the Church, Oliver Cowdery practiced law, but again joined the Latter-day Saints at Council Bluffs, Iowa late in 1849, where he was rebaptized. Just before rejoining the Church, he wrote to David Whitmer: "Let the Lord vindicate our characters and cause our testimony to shine, and then will men be saved in his kingdom" (Ludlow (1982), 339). He not only reiterated his firm testimony of the Book of Mormon, but testified of his presence when the Melchizedek Priesthood was restored in 1829. Many Latter-day Saints had been migrating to Salt Lake City since 1847. Because of the lateness of the season, Oliver Cowdery couldn't travel west. He went to live with David Whitmer in Richmond, Missouri, during the winter and died the following March at age 43.

Martin Harris was 46, twice the age of Joseph Smith, when the Book of Mormon was translated, which makes his support of Joseph Smith noteworthy. Earlier Joseph Smith, as a boy, had worked for and impressed Mr. Harris, who was a prosperous farmer and businessman in Palmyra. While he was the scribe in translating the Book of Mormon, he convinced Joseph Smith to allow him to take 116 pages of completed manuscript to show his wife. Somehow, the 116 pages became lost and in a revelation to Joseph Smith, Martin Harris was called a "wicked man" (D&C 3:12). Nevertheless, even though he was not allowed to translate, he financed the Book of Mormon. His loyalty to Joseph Smith resulted in his wife divorcing him. When the members of the Church left Kirtland, Harris remained behind and was not involved with the Church for thirty years. Martin Harris came to Utah in 1870 and often declared his testimony, including a dramatic affirmation in the Salt Lake Tabernacle, throughout the territory. His most powerful witness occurred on his deathbed in Clarkston, Utah in 1875. At nearly 93 years of age, he reiterated the truth of the visit of the angel and bore testimony of the divine origin of the Book of Mormon.

David Whitmer was excommunicated from the Church and never rejoined. In Richmond, Missouri, in 1888, he died, after having become a successful businessman, a respected citizen, and a mayor. He was the last of the witnesses to die. Hundreds of people visited him to hear his experience with the Book of Mormon plates and the angel. Some hoped to hear him renounce it, but he never did. A year before his death, he became annoyed by rumors that he had denied his testimony. He purchased advertising space in newspapers as far as Chicago and proclaimed, "It is recorded in the *American Cyclopedia* and the *Encyclopedia Britannica,* that I, David Whitmer, have denied my testimony as one of the Three Witnesses to the divinity of the Book of Mormon . . . . I will say once more to all mankind, that I have never at any time denied that testimony or any part thereof. I also testify to the world, that neither Oliver Cowdery nor Martin Harris ever at any time denied their testimony. Both died reaffirming the truth of the divine authenticity of the Book of Mormon" (Smith, (1963), 80).

Further Readings: Anderson (1980); Anderson (1987), 23–27; *EM* (1992), 214–16; 335–40; Reynolds (1997), 39–60.

CHAPTER FIVE

Book of Mormon "Problems"

5.1. Does a Doctrine and Covenants passage say there should only be three witnesses?

Over the years critics have tried to discredit the Book of Mormon in any way possible. They charge that since the Doctrine and Covenants (5:10–15) says only three witnesses would testify of the Book of Mormon, it was a false prophecy, since eight others also claimed to be witnesses. In context, the verses refer to the three witnesses to whom an angel showed the plates and who heard a voice from heaven declaring that the book was true. The Doctrine and Covenants verses do not preclude others who could see the plates under ordinary conditions. The critics ignore the Book of Mormon verses that predict more than three witnesses would be permitted to see the plates. Moroni stated the recipient of the records in the latter days would "be privileged [to] *show the plates unto those who will assist to bring forth this work; and* unto three shall they be shown by the power of God" (Ether 5:2–4; emphasis added. See also 2 Ne. 27:12–13).

5.2. Since the original plates are not available, isn't it logical to doubt the Book of Mormon?

The authenticity of any book is not dependent upon the availability of original documents. Not one original biblical manuscript exists either, yet millions believe in them as Holy Scriptures.

Despite lack of primary documents, both the Bible and Book of Mormon exist and are available for sincere study.

5.3. Does the reference to the people in the Book of Mormon touching Jesus contradict the Bible?

It is true, Jesus told Mary Magdalene, "Touch me not; for I am not yet ascended to my Father" (John 20:17). However, Jesus obviously visited His Father shortly thereafter. Later, in the same day, Jesus appeared in the midst of His apostles and said, "Behold my hands and my feet, that it is I myself: *handle me,* and see; for a spirit hath not flesh and bones, as ye see me have" (Luke 24:39–40; emphasis added). A few days later, the Savior invited Thomas to do the same (See John 20:26–29).

Sometime after His resurrection (the Book of Mormon is not clear on the exact time), Christ visited the Book of Mormon people, at which time He invited them to do likewise (See 3 Nephi 10:18–19; 11:1–3 and 19:1–5; Peterson (1995), 93; Ludlow (1976), 200). Thus, all doubt was removed from among the Nephites that He was, indeed, the Christ they had been told would come to the Eastern and Western Hemispheres.

5.4. Why does the Book of Mormon say that Jesus was born "in" Jerusalem?

The Book of Mormon does not say Jesus was born *in* Jerusalem, but *at* Jerusalem. The Book of Mormon also says it was "*the land* of our forefathers," not the city of our forefathers. Today, evidence has been found that the area around Jerusalem was referred to as the Land of Jerusalem (Griffith, 1993, 15–21). Bethlehem, being only five miles from Jerusalem, was certainly part of this area.

In addition, the 1828 Webster edition of the dictionary (used in Joseph Smith's day) or any current dictionary, says that the meaning of the word "at" includes "near," "by," and "next to," as well as "in." Since Alma was relating this prophecy in America, hundreds of years after their forefathers left Jerusalem, some may not have understood "Bethlehem," whereas they all would have heard of Jerusalem.

Joseph Smith certainly knew in what town Jesus was born, and must have often sung "O Little Town of Bethlehem" at Christmas as he grew up. He used the word Jerusalem because that's the word that was on the plates and the plates agree with the Bible. In the Old Testament, the "City of David" and "Jerusalem" are terms used synonymously beginning with King David's capture of Jerusalem from the Jebusites (2 Sam. 5:7, 9; 1 Chr. 11:5, 7; 2 Chr. 5:2; 1 Kings 8:1). Even in the New Testament the angel said, "For unto you is born this day in the city of David a Saviour, which is Christ the Lord" (Luke 2:11). In verse two of the same chapter, Bethlehem was referred to as the City of David, making it clear that Bethlehem was considered part of Jerusalem.

Thus, if an angel in the New Testament can refer to Jesus being born in Jerusalem (City of David), the Book of Mormon is also correct in saying Christ was born at (near) Jerusalem. (The best non-LDS source for information I have found on the City of David being Jerusalem is in the Protestant *Interpreter's Dictionary of the Bible.* Nashville: Abingdon Press, 1962, vol. 1:782.)

Further Reading: Hickenbothham (1995), 230.

5.5. Does the new Book of Mormon subtitle suggest it teaches a "different Jesus?"

In recent years, The Church of Jesus Christ of Latter-day Saints has added to the title of the Book of Mormon a subtitle—*Another Testament of Jesus Christ.* Certainly this clarification is appropriate, since a fundamental purpose of the book is to provide a second witness to the New Testament of Christ's reality and divinity. Some suggest that since "another" means "different,"

Mormons have actually admitted they worship a "different Jesus." However, the first meaning of "another" (including *Webster's Ninth New Collegiate Dictionary*) is "additional, one more." This latter definition is the intent of "Another Testament of Jesus Christ."

5.6. How can the modern French word "adieu" be spoken in the ancient Book of Mormon?

What the Book of Mormon word was in the original language we do not know. *Adieu* had international usage in Joseph Smith's day, as it does today. Since the Book of Mormon is a translation into English, it is appropriate to use common, everyday usage. Daniel H. Ludlow has pointed out that "there is a Hebrew word *Lehitra 'ot*, which has essentially the same meaning in Hebrew as the word *adieu* has in French. Both of these words are much more than a simple farewell; they include the idea of a blessing" (Ludlow, 1976, 163). Literally, *adieu* means "I commend you to God." Michael Hickenbotham has also pointed out that those who fault Joseph Smith for using a French word must, "in fairness, also criticize King James translators for using French words such as *tache* (Ex. 26:6, 11), *laver* (Ex. 30:18, 28), and *bruit* (Jer. 10:22; Nah. 3:19) meaning "mark", "wash", and "noise." These French words were popular in Elizabethan English (Hickenbotham (1995), 228).

Further Reading: A Sure Foundation (1988), 16.

5.7. Since "Christian" is a Greek word, how could it be used in the Book of Mormon?

It is true that the term "Christian" was first used in the Bible in A.D. 43, at Antioch (Acts 11:26), but why should that prevent it from being in the Book of Mormon? It is found in Alma 46:15, long before the Savior appeared. Book of Mormon people were constantly taught of the coming of Christ and thus referred to themselves as Christians. What the Nephite word was we do not know. "Christian" was an English word in 1829. As in the previous answer, Joseph was translating (as good translators should) into the vernacular of his day.

5.8. Isn't the Book of Mormon male name Alma a female name in Hebrew?

True, but recent research has found that Alma was also used as a male name. There are numerous names both male and female. In the Dead Sea Scrolls the words, "Alma, son of Judah" are found. (This scroll and its translation are on display at the Shrine of the Book museum in Jerusalem.) (Hickenbotham (1995), 229).

Further Reading: Nibley (1967), 194–96.

5.9. If Book of Mormon people were Hebrew, why did they write in a form of Egyptian?

Both languages are related, being Semitic. Israel was often occupied by Egypt, so the Jews had much exposure to the Egyptian language. Moses grew up in a royal Egyptian household, and Israelites lived in Egyptian captivity for four hundred years. There have always been close political, cultural, and commercial ties between these neighbors, i.e, Jacob's sons traveling to Egypt to buy grain. The Jews sometimes made alliances with the Egyptians.

Scholar Michael T. Griffith, who has studied ancient history and foreign languages at Haifa University in Israel, including the Standard Arabic and Egyptian dialects, made a thorough study of the historic ties between Egyptians and Israelites. To show the cooperation between ancient Israel and the Egyptians, Griffith quotes from a non-LDS Near Eastern Scholar, Robert F. Smith. He said, "Since the Israelites had close political, commercial and cultural ties with Egypt . . . and since this included Hebrew settlements in Egypt, it should not seem odd either that the Brass Plates of Laban were "engraved in Egyptian, nor that Nephi and his successors kept their records in Egyptian" (Griffith (1993), 40–42).

Furthermore, Jewish leaders sometimes wrote important documents in Egyptian. Egyptian idiomatic expressions appear in the Bible. The Savior spent time in Egypt as a boy. Remains of a Jewish temple have been found in Egypt. To presume that Book of Mormon people would not use some form of the Egyptian language is to be unaware of the history of Israeli and Egyptian interactions.

5.10. Does the Bible contradict the Book of Mormon concerning Christ's crucifixion?

Critics point out that Matthew 27:45 and Mark 15:33 speak of three hours of darkness during the time the Savior was on the cross. They feel the three days of darkness in the Book of Mormon is a discrepancy. The Book of Mormon did say, "there shall be no light *upon the face of this land* . . . for the space of three days" (Helaman 14:20; emphasis added). This phenomenon is *not* related to what happened in the Holy Land. The Book of Mormon account speaks of great catastrophic destructions in their land, causing the three days of darkness. Other events have occurred in history where earthquakes and volcanic eruptions with flying dust and ash have created periods of darkness (Hickenbotham (1995), 231).

Another discrepancy noted by critics is that the Bible says Jesus was on the cross between the sixth and ninth hours (Luke 23:44), whereas the Book of Mormon says it was "in the morning" (3 Ne. 10:9). The eight-hour time difference should have made the crucifixion take place around midnight in America. Faultfinders have charged that Joseph Smith slipped on this point because the Book of Mormon said morning. However, the hours were measured beginning with sunrise in biblical times. Therefore, the sixth to ninth hours started somewhere around noon in the Holy Land and it *would* be morning in the Western Hemisphere as the Book of Mormon relates (See Jack West, *Trial of the Stick of Joseph,* 1981).

5.11. Aren't magical devices, such as the Urim and Thummim, condemned by the Bible?

Some have been critical of Joseph Smith's claim of using the Urim and Thummim in the translation of the Book of Mormon, considering it a form of divination that the Bible condemns (Deut.18:9–14). While there is "false" divination which this verse refers to, the Bible has objects that are used for godly purposes, meaning that the Urim and Thummin was a legitimate object used for religious biblical purposes. Joseph Smith did state that with the plates, he received a breastplate containing an instrument, which he used in the translation process. The device, called a Urim and Thummim, meaning "lights and perfections" in Hebrew, is mentioned numerous times in the Bible in a positive way (Ex. 28:15, 30; Lev. 8:8; Num. 27:21; Deut. 33:8; 1 Sam. 28:6; Ezra 1:63; Neh. 7:65).

5.12. Why does the Book of Mormon use so much King James English?

Obviously, the original language of the Book of Mormon was not King James English. However, in the translation process, many King James words and expressions, which were the vernacular in Joseph Smith's day, were included. A good translation should reflect everyday usage of the audience it is intended for. The King James Bible was the most commonly used Bible in English speaking lands in the 1800s, and still remains a preferred Bible today, in spite of the dozens of new modern translations.

5.13. Why do many verses and chapters from the Bible appear in the Book of Mormon?

Some have suggested Joseph Smith was running short of ideas and thus turned to the Bible for more material. However, those persons involved with the Book of Mormon translation all relate that Joseph did not have a Bible or any reference material in his possession during the translation process. Therefore the biblical passages must have come from the plates. Biblical quotes in the Book of Mormon are almost all cross-referenced to the Bible in footnotes.

5.14. Is there an explanation for over 4,000 changes in the Book of Mormon?

First editions seldom, if ever, do not have errors. This is certainly true of books typeset from handwritten manuscripts, as was the Book of Mormon. Even with today's advanced publishing methods, trained writers, proofreaders, and word processors with spell and grammar checks, first editions have mistakes. The Book of Mormon manuscript given to the printer was a longhand copy in cursive made from another longhand copy. The manuscripts contained no punctuation. Evidently no proofreading was done, except what the printer did. Indeed, 4,000 errors seem few for a volume of such magnitude.

5.15. What is the nature of the changes in the Book of Mormon?

Almost every change was to correct grammatical, spelling, and typographical errors, as well as one clarification of doctrine. A critical edition of the Book of Mormon prepared by Royal Skousen is available through the Foundation for Ancient Research & Mormon Studies (F.A.R.M.S.). This work makes it easy for anyone to see every change that has been made in every Book of Mormon edition. As one studies Skousen's monumental work, one will see that many "errors" (corrected to reflect modern spelling) were actually the way people commonly spelled in those days. Many words "misspelled" in the early editions of the Book of Mormon actually coincided with the spelling in older versions of English. American English spelling was not yet standardized in the early 1800s. Still today, American spelling sometimes differs from the way words are written in England.

Every change in the Book of Mormon has been minutely scrutinized by friend and foe. Numerous commentaries have been written on the subject of Book of Mormon changes. These alterations have logical explanations, and almost every revision is trivial. One clarification change affects four verses and will be discussed in the next question.

A change in the most recent 1981 edition of the Book of Mormon caused a stir among some critics. The phrase "white and delightsome" was changed to "pure and a delightsome" (2 Ne. 30:6). However, "pure and a delightsome" was the phrase in the 1842 second edition. Thus, the 1981 correction was a restoration, instead of a change, reflecting what was intended by the Prophet Joseph Smith.

Elder Boyd K. Packer of the Council of Twelve has commented on complaints about Book of Mormon revisions: "[Critics] cite these changes . . . as though they themselves were announcing revelation, as though they were the only ones that knew of them . . . When properly reviewed, such corrections become a testimony *for*, not *against*, the truth of the book" (*Ensign*, May 1974, 94).

5.16. How can "the most correct of any book on earth" have so many alterations?

This description of the Book of Mormon by Joseph Smith does *not* say the book is infallible or inerrant, as some Christians say of the Bible. On the title page of the Book of Mormon, Moroni wrote: "if there are faults they are the mistakes of men; wherefore, condemn not the things of God." In fact Moroni, the last author of the Book of Mormon, lamented his imperfections and weakness in writing and prophesied that many "shall mock at our words" (Ether 12:25). Joseph Smith, who made most of the Book of Mormon corrections in his lifetime, knew of the errors. When he made his "most correct" statement in 1841, he obviously was referring to the message, the testimony of Jesus, the unique and clarifying doctrines. The power to change lives and motivate people to good works qualifies the Book of Mormon as "the most correct book." It is important to remember that the revisions did not change any doctrine or other meanings.

5.17. Did Egyptologist Charles Anthon deny giving written verification to Martin Harris?

Before Martin Harris became a scribe during the Book of Mormon translation, Joseph Smith had copied on paper some Reformed Egyptian inscriptions from the plates. Harris took this copy to New York City and was referred to Dr. Charles Anthon of Columbia College (now Columbia University). The accounts of the two men differ. Martin Harris said that Anthon gave him a certificate declaring the accuracy of the translation. However, when Dr. Anthon asked Harris how Joseph Smith received the plates, Harris replied, "An angel of God revealed it unto him." According to Harris's account, "[Mr. Anthon then took the certificate] and tore it to pieces, saying, that there were no such things now as ministering of angels, and that if I would bring the plates to him, he would translate them. I informed him that parts of the plates were sealed, and that I was forbidden to bring them. He replied 'I cannot read a sealed book.' I left him and went to Dr. [Samuel L.] Mitchell, who sanctioned what Professor Anthon had said respecting both the characters and the translation" (*HC,* 1:20).

In a letter to E. D. Howe, who published a book against the LDS Church in 1834, Dr. Anthon acknowledged the visit of Martin Harris and that he had given him a certificate. However, in 1841, Professor Anthon left another written account of his visit with Harris, "in which he contradicted himself" and said he had not given him a certificate. In both accounts, Anthon claimed he told Martin Harris that he was a victim of fraud (Ludlow, 1992, 1:43).

It seems more likely that Harris told the truth, rather than Anthon, since Anthon had a reputation to protect and he evidently did not want to admit to supporting something he knew so little about. Also, since his accounts are conflicting, there is reason to question them. On the other hand, Martin Harris, in addition to risking his good reputation, was searching for proof to determine if he should spend money and time helping Joseph Smith. He was a mature, prosperous, and respected businessman in Palmyra. Whatever happened between Harris and the two New York City scholars in February of 1828, Martin Harris came away a firm supporter of Joseph Smith. Harris had already been the prophet's scribe for a time, and remained true to his testimony as printed in the front of the Book of Mormon. His loyalty to Joseph Smith and the Book of Mormon is remarkable, since Martin Harris was later openly rebuked by the prophet. Harris lost 116 pages of the Book of Mormon manuscript and was not allowed to continue as scribe. Despite this chastisement, Harris financed the first edition of the Book of Mormon and testified of it until his dying day, at nearly 93 years of age, in Clarkson, Utah, in 1875.

Further Reading: Anderson (1980).

5.18. Why does the Book of Mormon claim to have the "fulness of the gospel," when some LDS doctrines are missing?

Various churches define words differently. To some, the word "Torah" means the first five Books of Moses. To others "Torah" also means the entire Old Testament. Both interpretations are correct. The first example is a narrow meaning; the second is a broad interpretation. We find various definitions of the word "sacrament" among churches. Protestants use a narrow meaning and have two sacraments. Catholics define the word more broadly and have seven sacraments. Saying Protestants do not have all the sacraments would be foolish for anyone since they believe only two are necessary.

Latter-day Saints do believe the Bible and the Book of Mormon contain the fulness of the gospel (Book of Mormon, Introduction, first sentence). The word "gospel" has both narrow and broad meanings. The narrow definition in *Webster's Ninth New Collegiate Dictionary* is "the message concerning Christ, the kingdom of God, and salvation." The broader definition in that dictionary is that "gospel" is the message or teachings of religious leaders.

The Book of Mormon uses the meaning that leans toward the narrow definition concerning Christ and salvation, as defined in the foregoing and other dictionaries. The Book of Mormon actually uses the definition that Christ taught during His ministry: "Behold, I have given unto you my gospel, and this is the gospel which I have given unto you—that I came into the world to do the will of my Father, because my Father sent me. And my Father sent me that I might be lifted up upon the cross; and after . . . I had been lifted up upon the cross, that I might draw all men unto me, that as I have been lifted up by men even so should men be lifted up by the Father, to stand before me, to be judged of their works, whether they be good or whether they be evil." The Savior continued listing repentance, baptism, reception of the Holy Ghost, and enduring to the end. Then He again said, "This is my gospel" (3 Ne. 27:13–21). Thus the Book of Mormon is true to its own definition of "gospel."

Further Readings: EM (1992) 2:530; Peterson and Ricks (1992), 29.

CHAPTER SIX
Changing Concepts

6.1. Since God doesn't change, how can one explain revisions in LDS doctrine and practice?

Parents need to treat each child differently, not necessarily because the parents change, but because each child is unique. Yes, God operates under eternal laws, but those laws allow for adaptability in what He expects from His children according to their needs and conditions.

Because God allows His children the freedom to choose between right and wrong, He at times adapts His requirements to fit their status and capacities. To claim God would not modify the way He relates to His children is to claim we know more about God than has, in fact, been revealed.

Sometimes the Lord responds to the mistakes His children make; at other times He responds to nurture their further growth. God gives His children "line upon line, precept upon precept" (2 Ne. 28:30; Isaiah 28:10, 13). The Bible and modern scripture support the idea of God changing His requirements as circumstances vary. Some examples follow.

1. In the days of the judges, the people insisted on a king. The Lord warned them of the danger of kings through the prophet Samuel. However, when the children of Israel persisted in their demand, God consented to their wishes and told Samuel to choose Saul to be their ruler (See 1 Sam. 8).

2. Before the days of Moses, God did not permit divorce. However, He allowed that prophet to grant divorce "because of the hardness of [the people's] hearts" (Matt. 19:8).

3. God said, "Thou shalt not kill." At other times He said, "Thou shalt utterly destroy" (Judges 21:11; 1 Samuel 15:3.).

4. God commanded the children of Israel to invade Canaan, (Numbers 13:1–2). They, however, were afraid and reluctant, and did not trust the Lord. He postponed their entry into the promised land 40 years (Num.14:33).

5. The word of the Lord came to ailing Hezekiah to get his "house in order; for thou shalt die and not live." However, the king pleaded with the Lord that he might not die. God then revoked His first decree and said to Isaiah: "Tell Hezekiah . . . I have heard thy prayer . . . I will heal thee . . . and I will add unto thy

days fifteen years" (2 Kings 20:1–6).

6. God, through the prophet Nathan, commanded David to build a temple (2 Sam. 7:4–5). Later, God changed His original instructions because of David's wickedness in committing adultery and murder. The Lord had Solomon construct the House of the Lord (1 Chr. 28:6).

7. God gave His people "an everlasting covenant" of circumcision (See Gen. 17:8–10). Later the requirement was lifted. (Acts 15).

8. When the children of Israel were incapable of living God's higher law, they received the lesser Mosaic law. During His earthly ministry, Christ again restored His higher law.

9. Paul taught that women should be silent and not teach (See 1 Cor. 14:34–35). At other times women missionaries labored with Paul, and some were prophetesses (Rom. 16:1–4; Phil. 4:2–3; 1 Cor. 11:5; Luke 2:36).

10. The Lord commanded Adam and Eve to practice animal sacrifice as a sign of His coming sacrifice for humanity (See Moses 5:4–8). This practice changed when the Savior sacrificed His life on the cross. Since

the Atonement fulfilled the ancient law, Christ expects from us another kind of oblation: "Ye shall offer for a sacrifice unto me a broken heart and a contrite spirit" (3 Ne. 9:20).

Today, this idea of God modifying His commandments to meet varying conditions is also found in modern scripture: "I, the Lord, command *and revoke, as seemeth me good*" (D&C 56:4; emphasis added).

Further Reading: Hickenbotham (1995), 66–68.

6.2. Why were blacks not given the priesthood in the Church before 1978?

Reasons for the priesthood restrictions on blacks "we believe are only known to God, and not to man," the Church declared in an official First Presidency statement (*Improvement Era,* February 1970, 71). "For my thoughts are not your thoughts, neither are your ways my ways, saith the Lord" (Isa. 55:8). In this life, Paul stated, we "see through a glass darkly" (1 Cor. 13:12).

Many Latter-day Saints considered the temporary ban on the priesthood similar to Christ's temporary denial of baptism of the Gentiles. This restriction was lifted by the Lord's revelation to Peter that the gospel was no longer to be limited to the Jews. With the conversion of Cornelius, all Gentiles received the opportunity to become members of Christ's church (Acts 10:15–28).

Although the Bible is virtually silent on the subject of race and skin color, many Church members took comfort in Christ's parable of the laborers, where the last hired received as much pay as the first workers (See Matt. 20:1–6). The Book of Mormon also gave promise to members of a day when blacks could hold the priesthood. "[The Lord] inviteth them all to come unto him and partake of his goodness; and he denieth none that come unto him, black and white . . . and all are alike unto God" (2 Ne. 26:33).

Most black members, of course, wanted the priesthood denial lifted, but they coped with the ban because of the blessings that the Church brought to their lives. One black member summed up his feelings by saying, "I guess when it all comes out in the end the important thing in God's Kingdom will not be who leads us there, but simply who gets there" (Alan Gerald Cherry, *It's You and Me, Lord,* 64). In 1976, Cherry was one of the first blacks to receive the priesthood.

Further Readings: Hickenbotham (1995), 61–63; *EM* (1992), 1:125–27.

6.3. What brought about giving the priesthood to black males and what was the reaction?

With ever-increasing numbers of blacks joining the LDS Church, especially in South America, President Spencer W. Kimball was inspired to ask the

Lord if the time was right to change the Church policy. On June 9, 1978, Church President Kimball
announced that all worthy males could now hold the
priesthood. After weeks of going to the Salt Lake
Temple to pray, at times when he could be alone, the
LDS prophet stated: "This revelation and assurance
came to me so clearly that there was no question
about it" (*Church News*, 6 January 1979, 4). At the
next general conference a vote of members present
unanimously approved the revelation (D&C, Official
Declaration—2).

Some felt the Church made changes because of
outside pressure. Such pressure had existed for
decades, even greater than it was in 1978. If this was
a factor, the Church would have made the change
much earlier.

This was truly a significant new revelation, and
almost all members of the Church were relieved and
accepted it gladly. Wire services sent the announce-
ment worldwide where there too, almost all response
was positive.

6.4. How did the LDS Church get into the practice of polygamy?

The practice of plurality of wives was revealed to
Joseph Smith by the Lord as early as 1831, but a
reluctant Joseph Smith did not make it public,
undoubtedly knowing the wrath that would result.

154

He did not put it into its present form until July 12, 1843 (see D&C 132).

Technically, *polygamy* is marriage in which a spouse of either sex may possess a plurality of mates simultaneously. Polyandry is the practice of wives having more than one husband at a time.

Besides believing the commandment came from the Lord, Latter-day Saints were also aware that at times, plural marriage was common among biblical leaders. Some patriarchs, prophets, and kings practiced it, including Abraham, Isaac, and Jacob. David had wives given him of God (2 Sam. 12:7, 8; see *Marriage, Plural* in the Topical Guide for other examples). However, the Lord was angry when the practice was abused by David (2 Sam. 12) and Solomon (Jacob 2:24). Only those committed to the highest standards of morality in the Bible and in the LDS Church were, at times, sanctioned to practice plurality of wives.

6.5. Why did the LDS Church stop the practice of plurality of wives?

For decades, the federal government had passed legislation aimed at stopping plural marriage. The government action was largely politically motivated (Larson (1958), 192–236). Latter-day Saints felt this action was unconstitutional, and hundreds of Church leaders and members were imprisoned for upholding their beliefs or had gone into exile, including the president of the Church at the time, John Taylor. After the Supreme Court upheld legislation that opposed plural marriage, government action against the Latter-day Saints intensified, including confiscation of property and disincorporating the Church. Latter-day Saints endured their trials, and the Lord brought relief.

Just as faithful Latter-day Saints believe plural marriage was instigated by the Lord early in the Church through the Prophet Joseph Smith, faithful Latter-day Saints also believe it was stopped by the Lord through their prophet Wilford Woodruff in 1890. Since then LDS prophets continue to sustain president Woodruff's revelation (See *Excerpts From Three Addresses* by President Wilford Woodruff regarding the Manifesto following D&C, Official Declaration—1). In the next conference of the church, members present voted unanimously to uphold it.

That monogamy is the rule, and plurality of wives the exception, has scriptural support. The Lord proclaimed early in the Book of Mormon, "There shall not any man among you have save it be one wife . . . Wherefore, this people shall keep my commandments . . . for if *I will,* saith the Lord of Hosts, raise up seed unto me, I will command my people; otherwise they shall hearken unto these things" (Jacob 2:27–30; emphasis added). The

Book of Mormon mentions plurality of wives a few times, but always practiced by wicked people. Unless otherwise commanded, that lifestyle is without the Lord's approval. A man "should have one wife" (D&C 49:16).

The first half of Section 132, dealing with eternal marriage, speaks of a husband and one wife. Several times the verses speak of "a"wife (See verses 15–26). Some claim that Section 132, when it speaks of "an everlasting covenant," means that plural marriage should never have been done away with. This is erroneous. Years before section 132 was written, several other references to "the everlasting covenant" talk about the restored gospel (see D&C 45:9; 49:9; 66:2; 76:101). Earlier usage of "a *new* and everlasting covenant" also means the restored gospel (See 27:5; 79:1; 101:39; 138:19, 25).

Those who claim that plural marriage should never have been abolished claim that President John Taylor had a "revelation" in 1885 that makes this clear. However, a copy of this "revelation" does not mention plural marriage at all, but says "the new and everlasting covenant" should never be done away with. As was shown in the previous paragraph, this expression refers to the whole gospel and not plurality of wives.

The issue of plural marriage is another example of the principle that the "Lord commands and revokes," at times, as addressed in question 6.1. LDS apostle Bruce R. McConkie stated: "Plural marriage is not essential to salvation or exaltation" (McConkie, 1976, 578). Apostle James E. Talmage also said, "Plurality of wives was an incident, never an essential" (Talmage (1930), 89).

Further Reading: Ludlow (1992), 3:1091; Scharffs (1989), 207–17; Winwood (1995), 26–28.

6.6. Did the practice of plural marriage continue after the Manifesto?

Church leaders worded the Manifesto to meet the political realities of the day. It required Latter-day Saints to "refrain from contracting any marriages forbidden by the law of the land." The Church intended that existing marriages would remain intact, since breaking up of families started before the Manifesto would cause untold suffering among the Saints. Federal officials, on the other hand, wanted these existing marriages revoked, and bitter conflicts between the Church and state continued. The government eventually backed off, also realizing that forcing fatherless families would cause more social problems than society could properly handle.

Some in the Church interpreted the Manifesto to not include new plural marriages outside the United States, where polygyny was not against the laws of the land. President Joseph F. Smith issued a second Manifesto in 1905 to stop all such plural marriages. A few new marriages were performed, but soon the practice of plurality of wives in the LDS Church faded away as participants died. A few splinter groups still practice this lifestyle today, but members of the LDS Church who practice plural marriage or even advocate it are excommunicated.

6.7. Did Brigham Young teach that Adam was God the Father?

A printed account quotes Brigham Young as saying, "Adam is our father and our god and the only god with whom we have to do"(*Journal of Discourses,* 1:50–51). However, later in the same speech, President Young is quoted as saying there were three that created the earth: "Elohiem, Jehovah, and Michael." To Latter-day Saints, these three names refer to God the Father, Jesus, and Adam. Thus the man Adam, before he came to this earth, was in a sense "*a* god," but *not* "God *the* Father." As first patriarch of the earth, Adam also has presiding seniority over all other prophets, and is directly accountable to Jesus Christ. Also, LDS belief maintains those ancient prophets such as Abraham, Isaac, Jacob, and perhaps others, including the man Adam, have achieved godhood status by now. Thus, in LDS doctrine, the man Adam may correctly be referred to as *a* god, but not God, who was the Father of Jesus Christ and the spiritual father of all humankind, including Adam and Eve.

A good case can be made that Brigham Young was not quoted correctly or was misunderstood. There are other occasions when President Young spoke of Adam being created by God the Father. "The Gospel tells us that we are the sons and daughters of that God whom we serve. Some say we are the children of Adam and Eve, so we are, and *they are the children of our Heavenly Father*" (*Journal of Discourses* 13:31). "We believe that [God] made Adam after His own image and likeness, as Moses testifies." (10:211). Brigham Young also taught "Adam was as conversant with His Father, who placed him upon this earth, as we are conversant with our earthly parents. The Father frequently came to visit His son Adam, and talked with and walked with him" (9:148). On another occasion, Brigham Young played down the idea of trying to understand the origin of Adam when he said, the subject "does not immediately concern yours or my welfare" (Hale, 1982, 7:4).

Incorrect transcriptions could also have caused Brigham Young to be misunderstood. A clerk, George Watt, recorded in Pitman shorthand many sermons that were later printed in the *Journal of Discourses*. He then transcribed them into longhand. The hand-written copy was then typeset by hand and printed in England, not as an official Church publication, but as a private venture. The typesetters threw away the shorthand and longhand versions, as most printers do to avoid paper piling up. The original versions of the controversial Adam/God speech have not been found. When a long letter is dictated to a very competent secretary, the person dictating almost always has to correct the first draft. Making mistakes when taking dictation is common for secretaries. George Watt most likely made mistakes as he wrote long speeches hours at a time in shorthand, without having the chance to stop the speaker and ask him to repeat his last sentence, as secretaries often do.

LDS researcher Elden Watson has read all of the journals he could find—nearly fifty—where others who were in attendance commented on the Brigham Young speech given on April 9, 1852 (see *Journal of Discourses* 1:51–52). Watson points out that Wilford Woodruff, an Apostle at the time who later became the fourth LDS president, made notes on the sermon. President Woodruff's version contains additional material at the critical point of the talk that is not in the *printed* version. Also under the same date, Samuel Holister Rogers journal has similar additional material. Watson has said, "although reconstructing exactly what the missing words were is not possible, the stenographer or printers clearly omitted something from the *Journal of Discourses* account. The two journals contained only outlined ideas and not verbatim statements." If just one or a few words are missing from the printed account (a distinct possibility in view of the forgoing mentioned journals), what Brigham Young meant could be completely different.

Some have suggested that Brigham Young used the word "Adam" as a title for God. Those who advocate this idea quote the words of Paul when he said, "The *first man Adam* was made a living soul; the *last Adam* was made a quickening spirit . . . the Lord from heaven" (1 Cor. 15:45–47; emphasis added). Paul is speaking of two persons with the same title: the man Adam as the first of the human race, and another Adam (Jesus Christ). Thus, Adam is one of many titles used for Jesus Christ, and perhaps a title for God the Father.

Furthermore, another title Jesus often used to refer to Himself was "Son of Man." This reads "Son of Adam" in New Testament Aramaic texts. Who, then, is the "Adam" that Jesus was the son of? Christ certainly was not the Son of Adam and Eve, the world's first mortals. The Bible makes it clear that Jesus was the Son of God the Father. Thus, Christ's many references to being "Son of Adam" could mean that the title "Adam" also refers to God the Father. This does not make the man Adam the same as the God Adam. Brigham Young was familiar with the man Adam's subordinate role to God the Father and His Son Jesus Christ.

Advocates of Adam being a title also quote Elder Bruce R. McConkie. In a church-wide fireside in

1985, Elder McConkie spoke of the new editions of the LDS scriptures. He noted a correction that his committee made in Abraham 1:3 of the Pearl of Great Price: "They changed a single letter, to agree with an older manuscript and a new doctrinal meaning emerged." What once said "Adam, *our* first father" is now "Adam, *or* first father" (*Ensign,* Dec.1985, 59). This also suggests that Adam is a title and not a name. Latter-day Saints also know that Michael is the actual premortal name of the man Adam, making the word Adam a title (See D&C 27:11; 128:21).

Whether Brigham Young was misunderstood, misquoted, or simply wrong, it is certain that the man Adam is different from God the Father in LDS doctrine.

Further Readings: Robinson (1991), 18–21; Winwood (1995), 53–55.

CHAPTER SEVEN

Visits from Heaven

7.1. How can one believe the First Vision, since such an event has never occurred in history?

There was a similar happening at the stoning of Christ's follower, Stephen, who "being full of the Holy Ghost, looked up steadfastly into heaven, and saw the glory of God, and Jesus standing on the right hand of God" (Acts 7:55). Also at the baptism of Jesus and later on the Mount of Transfiguration, the voice of the Father came from heaven stating "This is my beloved Son, in whom I am well pleased" (Matt. 3:17; See also Matt. 17:5). These words are similar to the words the Father spoke when He introduced His Son, Jesus Christ, to Joseph Smith in 1820 (See Joseph Smith—History 1:17).

It is true that no biblical account is exactly like the First Vision event, where both the Father and the Son speak directly and in person to one of their prophets on the same occasion. Of course, not all accounts of God's dealing with His children on earth are available. There possibly were similar happenings.

Perhaps such a rare, and possibly unique, theophany (visual manifestation of Deity) was essential to the Restoration. It proved false the Trinitarian idea that existed at the time God restored the Church through Joseph Smith. When one realizes the erroneous theology about Deity that was preached at the time, one can understand why God and Christ would both appear. This First Vision underscored the separateness of the Godhead taught in the Bible.

Further Readings: Ludlow (1991) 2:515–516; Peterson and Ricks (1992) 158, 166–167.

7.2. Since Satan can appear as an angel of light, is this what Joseph Smith saw?

Critics often change their arguments, attempting to show that the First Vision could not have happened but arguing that if it did, it was of satanic origin. They quote 2 Corinthians 11:14, which states that Satan can appear as an "angel of light." However, it is clear in this passage that he disguises himself as such in an attempt to give himself credibility. This does not mean that all appearances of beings clothed in light are satanic. There are numerous biblical examples of light associated with deity. When the Lord came at the time of Paul's conversion, "there shined round about him a light from heaven" (Acts 9:3). "God is light" (1 John 1:5). "[God is the] Father of lights" (James 1:17). God speaking to Moses from the burning bush is another example of light associated with Deity.

Further Reading: Gibson (1995), 50–52.

7.3. Is it true that there was no religious revival in Palmyra, as Joseph Smith claimed?

Joseph Smith merely said there was "in the *place* [not town] where we lived an unusual excitement on the subject of religion," and it "became general among all sects in that *region* of country. Indeed, the whole *district of the country* seemed affected by it" (Joseph Smith—History 1:5; emphasis added). We have no record of Joseph Smith saying there was a revival in Palmyra. He did not describe what he meant by "religious excitement," "place where I lived," "whole district of the country," nor did he identify a precise period when all these events took place, or how he learned about these developments (See Backman (1980), 79).

Dr. Milton V. Backman, Jr., who has done extensive research on this issue, did find that there was a Methodist camp meeting that took place near Palmyra in 1820. This could have sparked Joseph Smith's questions about religion. Since circuit riding preachers visited small towns for a day or more in those days, one or more of them could have motivated Joseph Smith to seek religious answers by telling him of nearby camp meetings. In any event, there is no question that in the years 1819–1820 there were many revivals in western New York, which subsequently has been called the "burned over district" by historians, since there was so much religious fighting among religious leaders. Scholars also refer to this period of religious arousal as "the second great awakening." The period of the original "Great Awakening" in American history occurred in Kentucky two decades earlier (see Cross, 1950). There were many revivals within fifty miles of Palmyra, and at least six within twenty miles of where the Smiths lived (See Backman (1980), 79).

In his history, Joseph Smith described himself in his youth as "mingling with all kinds of society. . . [I] sometimes associated with jovial company, etc., not consistent with that character which ought to be maintained by one who was called of God as I had been. But this will not seem very strange to any one . . .acquainted with my native cheery temperament" (Joseph Smith—History 1:28). In Joseph Smith's earliest known account of the First Vision (1832), he stated that he had been engaged for two or three years in a quest for religious truth. During that time he certainly visited other communities, especially when he heard they were involved with religious happenings. These camp meetings were *the* place to be at that time. Dr. Backman's extensive study concluded, "Indeed, the Mormon Prophet penned a brief but reliable descrip-

tion of the environment [in which he lived]"
(Backman, 1980, 89).

7.4. Do the eight versions of the First Vision contradict each other?

The earliest known written account of the First
Vision written in Joseph Smith's own handwriting,
dated 1832, is the most detailed. Seven other versions, written by scribes or those who heard Joseph
Smith relate the vision, are available (Backman,
1980). The different accounts are surprisingly similar,
especially when one realizes they were recorded sometimes years apart. Each account has some different
detail, but no contradictions. All eight of the known
accounts written during the prophet's lifetime speak
of his quest to know which church (if any) was right.
They also mention his searching the scriptures, his
prayer, and the appearance of Deity. All accounts but
the first speak of two personages. The prophet never
polished the first to a point for publication. Joseph
Smith's scribes, or those who heard the Prophet,
wrote the other seven versions, paraphrasing them
into their own words, since they relied on their memory. If all the accounts were identical, then one might
be suspicious of fraud or collusion. For a comparison
of the accounts, read James B. Allen's, "Eight
Contemporary Accounts of Joseph Smith's First
Vision—What do we learn from them?"

(*Improvement Era,* Apr. 1970, 4–13).

Further Readings: Allen (1970), 4–13; Bushman (1968), 86–91; Jessee (1984), 515–576: Scharffs (1989), 300; Winwood (1995), 40–43.

7.5. Why did Joseph's earliest account of the First Vision mention only Jesus?

This earliest account is the only version that does not specifically mention both God the Father and His Son Jesus Christ appearing to Joseph Smith. The instructions Joseph Smith received were from Jesus, except when God the Father introduced Him saying, "This My Beloved Son. Hear Him!" This earliest known account does not contradict later versions; it merely lacks the clarity on this point that later portrayals of the First Vision contain.

Further Reading: Backman (1980).

7.6. Why is the First Vision not related in the Church until the twentieth century?

It is not correct to say no one proclaimed the First Vision until the twentieth century. A number of instances can be found, some in the *Journal of Discourses* (see Scharffs (1989), 305–306 for examples). It is true, however, that in printed sermons available from the first seventy-five years of the LDS Church, recitation of the First Vision was infrequent. There is no way of measuring how many First Vision

recitals were made by missionaries and in local sermons, which were not recorded.

Although Church members cautiously told the
Prophet's sacred experiences at first, their reality does
not depend on frequent repetition. "There is a corol-
lary operating—an inverse law of sacredness—which
dictates that the highest gifts will be reported guard-
edly and reverently." (Reynolds (1982), 223).

7.7. Did Joseph Smith claim in an account of the First Vision that all Christians are corrupt?

Joseph Smith's First Vision was a result of want-
ing to know which church to join (see Joseph
Smith—History 1:18). He was surprised when the
Savior replied that he should join none of them.
Since the Lord planned to restore the fullness of the
gospel through Joseph Smith, He would not want
him joining other churches. This is different from
calling all Christians today (or even then) corrupt.
Nor is this saying that there is not much good being
done today by many Christians and their churches.
(See also questions 1.5, 1.6, 1.8, chapter one, for the
LDS Church's official position about other religions.)

Christ continued His instruction to young
Joseph, making clear it was *the man-made creeds* that
"were an abomination in his sight." These creeds
became part of Christianity when monarchs politically

mandated them hundreds of years after Christ's ministry. The Savior added that professors [of those creeds] were all corrupt, that: "they draw near to me with their lips, but their hearts are far from me, they teach for doctrines the commandments of men, having a form of godliness, but they deny the power thereof" (Joseph Smith—History 1:19).

It makes sense that Jesus Christ would be angry with those who were substituting nonbiblical teachings and creeds of men for His holy scriptures. Also to "deny the power" (need for Christ's authority) was offensive to the Savior, since He and His apostles emphasized the necessity of authority during their mortal ministry (see Eph. 2:19–21; 4:11–14). Leaders of churches in Joseph Smith's day denied any need for power (direct authority) from God, a fact that gives credence to the account in the First Vision, which points out that many churches were denying the need for any direct authority from God.

Further Reading: Ludlow (1992), 1:343.

7.8. Was Joseph Smith known for "money digging" before claiming he found gold plates?

For a few months in 1826, Joseph Smith did work for Josiah Stoal helping him dig for silver. The twenty-one-year-old Joseph needed work to help feed his impoverished family. At the time he worked for Stoal, Joseph Smith had already experienced contacts with the

Angel Moroni and was shown the Book of Mormon plates. This was also six years after the Prophet's First Vision. Joseph Smith's mother's history said: "Joseph tried to convince Mr. Stoal to give up the project."

In Joseph Smith's day, seeking treasure was common in his locale. In the northeastern U.S. during the 1820s, digging for treasure was not disreputable. The *Palmyra Herald* on 24 July 1822 stated, "We could name, if we pleased, at least five hundred respectable men, who do, in the simplicity and sincerity of their hearts verily believe that immense treasure lies concealed upon our green mountains. Many . . . have been for a number of years, most industriously and perseveringly engaged in digging it up" (Mulder and Mortensen, 33).

Joseph Smith admitted having faults. The Lord took Joseph Smith, a man innocently caught up in the superstition of his day, and turned him into a mighty Prophet of the Restoration. He said himself, "I am a rough stone. The sound of the hammer and chisel was never heard on me until the Lord took me in hand. I desire the learning and wisdom of heaven alone" (Smith, 1902, 5:423).

Further Readings: Roberts (1930), 26–27; McConkie (1998), 49.

7.9. Does the lack of an exact date of restoration make the Melchizedek Priesthood doubtful?

The LDS Church has documented dates for just about every important aspect of the Restoration of the gospel. Not knowing a particular date has nothing to do with an event's reality. Researchers have not identified a single date in Christ's life or the lives of His apostles, but this does not keep us from accepting the Savior. If Mormonism is the fraud some critics claim it is, why did not Joseph Smith or another follower make up a date? It is true that up to now, the date of the restoration of the Melchizedek Priesthood has not been found. However, the occurrence is narrowed by some historians to the latter part of May or early June.

Further Reading: Bushman (1984), 22.

7.10. Could Oliver Cowdery have falsified his testimony so he could return to the Church?

Would Oliver Cowdery want to return to an organization if he thought it was a scam? He received no worldly benefits by returning, no leadership positions. Historian Richard Anderson, who has spent many years studying the life of Oliver Cowdery and the other witnesses to the Book of Mormon, has found him to be a man of highest integrity (Anderson, 1990). In a letter written by Oliver Cowdery to his brother-in-law, Phinias Young, two years before he decided to rejoin Mormonism, he said he was with Joseph Smith when Peter, James, and

John restored the Melchizedek priesthood (*Ensign*, Feb. 1977, 78).

Next to Joseph Smith's family, Oliver, perhaps more than any other living person, would know whether the LDS Prophet was what he claimed to be. Oliver, who felt the Church had treated him wrongly, had every reason and opportunity to expose Mormonism if he had not known for a surety that The Church of Jesus Christ of Latter-day Saints was true and of divine origin.

7.11. How come only Latter-day Saints speak of the mysterious Melchizedek ?

What seems mysterious is that seldom does any Christian religion even mention this biblical prophet—even those who claim the Bible is infallible and inerrant. The apostle Paul spoke emphatically of the importance of Melchizedek and reaffirmed David's great Messianic Psalm, which speaks of Melchizedek (Psalms 110:4). Paul quoted Christ, "Thou art a priest for ever after the order of Melchizedec" (Heb 5:6). Paul devoted three chapters (Heb. 5–7) to pointing out, among other things, that Melchizedek was a priest of the most high God, who blessed Abraham—a great man to whom even the patriarch Abraham paid tithes (Heb. 7:4; Gen. 14:18). These few biblical verses underscore the need for more information concerning this prophet, much of which is provided in the Book of Mormon and the Doctrine and Covenants.

Melchizedek is considered mysterious because in Hebrews 7:3, Paul states that Melchizedek is "without father, without mother, without descent, having neither beginning of days, nor end of life." Scholars have often interpreted this to mean that Melchizedek had no parents. The Book of Mormon clarifies this point by saying that it is the Melchizedek Priesthood that is "without beginning of days or end of years" (Alma 13:7).

Since the doctrine of Melchizedek Priesthood is biblical and The Church of Jesus Christ of Latter-day Saints is alone in claiming to possess it, this is further evidence of the truthfulness of the work restored by the Father and His Son Jesus Christ through the Prophet Joseph Smith.

Further Reading: McConkie (1966), 431–437.

CHAPTER EIGHT
Allegations Clarified

8.1. Does much LDS doctrine conflict with historic Christianity?

The answer to this question depends on which part of historic Christianity is involved. If the kind of Christianity referred to is after the second century A.D., the answer is yes. However, if historic Christianity means the New Testament times and several decades following Christ's ministry, many parallels are found between Christian practices at that time and what The Church of Jesus Christ of Latter-day Saints believes today. An excellent study of what early Christians believed is found in a non-LDS book called *Early Christian Doctrine* by J. N. D. Kelley, published by Harper and Row. Questions 2.1 and 2.2 in chapter two show that Latter-day Saints are closer to biblical teachings than today's other churches.

8.2. Do Latter-day Saints believe Jesus was begotten of the Father instead of the Holy Ghost?

Latter-day Saints believe that God the Father is the Father of Jesus Christ, and the Holy Ghost was also a factor. Most other Christians believe the Holy Ghost "conceived Jesus Christ," as stated in *Book of Common Prayer* (cited in Hickenbotham (1995), 95). The Bible, however, supports the LDS interpretation. Luke records an angel saying, "Fear not, Mary: for thou hast found favor with God . . .thou shalt conceive in thy womb, and bring forth a son, and shalt call his name Jesus. He shall be great, and shall be called *the Son of the Highest*" (Luke 1:30–32; emphasis added).

When Mary asked how this was possible since she was a virgin, the angel answered, "The Holy Ghost shall come upon thee, *and the power of the Highest* shall overshadow thee: therefore also *that holy thing which shall be born of thee shall be called the Son of God*" (verse 35; emphasis added). The Bible uses the term "highest" to refer to God the Father (Luke 1:76; 6:35–36).

Many biblical passages also call Jesus the Son of God, never son of the Holy Ghost (John 20:17; 2 John 1:3). Other New Testament passages also refer to Jesus as the "only begotten of the Father" (John 1:14, 18; 3:16; 1 John 4:9). When early church leaders debated the Nicene Creed in A.D. 325, it is interesting to note that in the final version they declare Jesus as "the only begotten son of God." Latter-day Saints agree with this part of the creed.

Today's mainstream Christian interpretation stems from the verse that says Mary was "found with child of the Holy Ghost" and "that which is conceived in her is of the Holy Ghost"(Matt. 1:18, 20). However, as seen in the previous scriptures, the Matthew account is true, but incomplete. The Holy Ghost is involved when God the Father deals with mortals. At the stoning of Stephen we are told, "he, being full of the Holy Ghost, looked up stedfastly into heaven, and saw the glory of God and Jesus standing on the right hand of God" (Acts 7:55). Three of the Gospels also say that at the baptism of Jesus, the Holy Ghost descended upon Jesus, and God the Father spoke from heaven and said, "Thou art my beloved Son; in thee I am well pleased" (Luke 3:22). In the same sense that the Holy Ghost gives a spiritual dimension when God deals with mortals (Luke 1:67), so was the Holy Ghost's involvement with Mary.

Further Readings: Hickenbotham (1995), 95–96; *EM* (1992), 2:673; 2:729; 2:863; 4:1510; Peterson and Ricks 129–131.

8.3. Do Latter-day Saints believe God had an affair with Mary?

The official LDS view is answered in the previous question. However, some LDS faultfinders claim that Latter-day Saints teach God had a sexual encounter with Mary. In a recent movie, "The Mormon Puzzle," made by a large Protestant group, BYU's Dean of Religious Instruction, Robert Millet, was asked this question. Dr. Millet emphatically replied, "How the conception of Mary was accomplished we do not know." In conversations with LDS General Authorities, this author was also told that Latter-day Saints have no doctrine concerning the method of procreation on the deity level.

8.4. Does the LDS Church teach that Jesus was married?

Neither the Bible, other LDS scriptures, nor official LDS statements are clear whether Jesus was married. On the other hand, LDS doctrine does not declare that Jesus was *not* married, as do many Protestants and Catholics. There has been some speculation by non-Mormons, LDS members and leaders, including Brigham Young on this subject, but such ideas are not officially part of the Church. Some non-LDS books argue that Jesus was married (Phipps, 1970). Since Latter-day Saints place great emphasis on families continuing into the eternities, Jesus being married is a possibility. (See also next question.)

Further Readings: Griffith (1994), 101–108; *EM* (1992), 2:961.

8.5. Do Latter-day Saints believe God is married and mortals have a Mother in Heaven?

Today there is a trend to remove masculine references in our language, including any mention of

God as a male in some new revisions of the Bible. Since its early days, LDS Church doctrine has included the idea that God the Father has a wife. Thus, there is no need to change all the biblical male references to God into a neuter form. Latter-day Saint doctrine states God has an equally important wife.

Although the Bible and the Book of Mormon do not specifically teach a Mother in heaven concept, it is suggested in the scriptures. Latter-day Saints believe the Bible makes a strong case for eternal marriage with such biblical passages as "Neither is the man without the woman, neither the woman without the man, in the Lord" (1 Cor. 11:11; see chapter two, question 2.2). In Genesis we read, "And God said, Let *us* make man in our own image, after our likeness: and let them have dominion . . . over all the earth . . . So God created man in his own image, in the image of God created he him, *male and female* created he *them*" (Gen. 1:26–27; emphasis added). It is possible that since God created male and female in His image that this verse means God patterned the first earthly couple after His own heavenly marriage.

In 1909, the First Presidency, under Joseph F. Smith, issued a statement on the origin of man that teaches "man, as spirit, was begotten and born of heavenly parents." However, as early as 1839, Joseph Smith taught the idea that was the inspiration for a hymn by Eliza R. Snow, "O My Father," which Latter-day Saints learn, sing, quote, and cherish. LDS president Wilford Woodruff called this song "a revelation" (*EM*, 1992, 2:961).

> In the heav'ns are parents single?
> No, the thought makes reason stare!
> Truth is reason; truth eternal
> Tells me I've a mother there.
> When I leave this frail existence,
> When I lay this mortal by,
> Father, Mother, may I meet you
> In your royal courts on high?
> (Hymn no. 292)

8.6. Does the Church teach "As man now is God once was, as God now is man may become"?

This couplet is attributed to Lorenzo Snow, who became the fifth president of the LDS Church. The latter part of the saying, "as God now is, man may become" is a definite LDS doctrine, not only because leaders have taught this deification of man concept, but because the principle has solid biblical support. God said that after the Fall, Adam and Eve became "as one of us" (Gen. 3:22). During His mortal ministry, Christ repeated this Old Testament doctrine when He called all humans gods (See John 10:34; Ps. 82:6). See other scriptures and quotes for support on this issue by many non-LDS leaders in question 1.12, chapter one.

However, the meaning of the first part of the

maxim, "As man now is, God once was," is not as clear as the second part. To support the idea that God at least had a mortal experience similar to His son Jesus Christ, perhaps in eons past, Joseph Smith referred to Christ's own statement: "The Son can do nothing of himself, but what he seeth the Father do: for what things soever [the Father] doeth, these also doeth the Son likewise" (John 5:19).

Stephen E. Robinson, in the *Encyclopedia of Mormonism*, said: "The Father became the Father at some time before 'the beginning' as humans know it, by experiencing a mortality similar to that experienced on earth. There has been speculation among some Latter-day Saints on the implications of this doctrine, but nothing has been revealed to the Church about conditions before 'the beginning' as mortals know it. The important points of the doctrine for Latter-day Saints are that God and humans are the same species, but at different stages of development in a divine continuum, and that the Heavenly Father and Mother are the heavenly pattern, model, and example of what mortals can become through obedience to the gospel."

"Knowing that we are the literal offspring of Heavenly Parents and that we can become like those parents through the gospel of Jesus Christ is a wellspring of religious motivation. With God as the literal Father and with humans having the capacity to become like Him, the basic religious questions 'Where did I come

from?' 'Why am I here?' and 'What is my destiny?' are
fundamentally answered" (Ludlow, 1992, 2:548–50).

In press interviews, reporters asked President
Gordon B. Hinckley if the Church believed that God
was once a man. President Hinckley indicated that
this is not an important issue that we emphasize in
the Church, and details of God's earlier condition we
do not know (*Time,* 4 Aug. 1997, 56). Latter-day
Saints believe the words of the Savior when He said
in His great intercessory prayer to His Father, "This
is life eternal, that they might know thee the only true
God and Jesus Christ, whom thou has sent" (John
17:3). A goal of Latter-day Saints is to grow in their
understanding and love for God the Father and His
Son Jesus Christ. However, as President Hinckley
cautioned, Latter-day Saints and others should not
speculate beyond what has been revealed.

LDS doctrine teaches that although humans are
of God's species and can become more like Him, there
will never be a time when we will not be accountable
to the members of the Godhead. Latter-day Saints do
not enthrone themselves in God's place. The possibility of achieving godhood (lowercase "g") is different
from Godhead. Christ spoke of this concept when He
said, "The disciple is not above his master: but every
one that is perfect shall be as his master" (Luke 6:40).
LDS doctrine declares that all the inhabitants of the
earth and God are coeternal (without beginning and

without end). Few details have been revealed.

8.7. Is church attendance more important to Mormons than a relationship with Christ?

Latter-day Saints do stress church attendance, but that does not mean Jesus is less important in their lives. To Latter-day Saints, going to church *is* vital and the result usually brings a person closer to Jesus Christ. Member involvement gives Latter-day Saints opportunities and incentives to live Christlike lives. To Latter-day Saints, the Church is a means to an end. The immediate purpose of the Church is to teach and encourage members to be decent, honorable, and law-abiding, and to be a positive influence on society.

8.8. Did Jesus Christ even have a Church?

Some insist Jesus did not organize a Church. Christ had followers, leaders, and rules. That certainly constitutes an organization. The Savior taught that the Church should resolve disputes (Matt. 18:17). That the Lord had a church is shown when he told Peter, "Upon this rock I will build my church" referring to Himself and revelation (Matt. 16:18). "The Lord added to the church daily" is another verse that supports this fact (Acts 2:47). After Christ's death, Peter was given a revelation from the Lord to allow non-Jews to become members of the Church (Acts 10: 15–28). Another verse states, "Is any sick among you?

let him call the elders of the church" (James 5:14).

8.9. Are Latter-day Saints taught not to worship Christ?

The Bible and Book of Mormon teach believers to worship God and Christ (3 Ne. 11:17; 2 Ne. 25:29). LDS apostle Bruce R. McConkie did caution against emphasizing Christ at the expense of other members of the Godhead. Doing so might prevent a person from keeping the full gospel in perspective, but that God and Christ should not be worshiped is a wrong interpretation. Latter-day Saints pray to the Father in the name of Jesus Christ. LDS apostles are special witnesses of Jesus Christ and encourage worship of the Savior and God the Father. "Believe in Christ and deny him not; and Christ is the Holy One of Israel; wherefore ye must . . . *worship* him with all your might, mind, and strength, and with your whole soul" (2 Nephi 25:29).

Further Readings: Griffith (1994), 65–67; Robinson (1991), 3, 13, 114.

8.10. Do Latter-day Saints testify of Joseph Smith and not Jesus Christ?

In reality, most Mormons do both, acknowledging Jesus as our divine Savior and Joseph Smith as the first great and noble Prophet of this last dispensation. No serious Latter-day Saint would ever claim for Joseph Smith an equality with our Lord and Savior, much less a superiority. Joseph Smith and his successors, as well as members of the LDS Church, have brought millions of people to the Lord Jesus Christ who might otherwise not have known Him.

8.11. Why wasn't the gospel of Jesus Christ on the earth until Joseph Smith came along?

Actually, Latter-day Saints believe the Lord gave the gospel to Adam and Eve, and it has been on the earth intermittently ever since. Periods of mass apostasy occurred following each time Christ's Church was on the earth. This was also the case after the Savior's earthly ministry in the Holy Land and after his visit in America. In Palestine, people put the Apostles to death. At first, Barnabas and Paul were added to the Twelve, but soon so many apostles were killed that getting together for replacements was impossible. Doctrines and leadership positions of the Church were dropped or changed. New nonbiblical ideas were added. Then a period known as the Dark Ages set in. With tyrannical monarchs and monopolistic state churches established, a restoration was not possible.

With the establishment of the United States of America, separation of church and state became the constitutional law of the land, and religious liberty was guaranteed. The open frontier situation that existed in early America helped enable new religious ideas to flourish. Those with unpopular beliefs could flee from those who persecuted them. This provided an opportunity for Christ's Church to again be restored to earth and flourish—The Church of Jesus Christ of Latter-day Saints.

Further Reading: McConkie (1998), 19–21.

8.12. If Joseph Smith restored Christ's Church, why did he join the Freemasons?

The consensus view I find in reading about Masons and talking to its members is that most adherents claim Masonry is not a religion, but a fraternal order. Scholars Donald Q. Cannon, Mervin B. Hogan and Kenneth W. Godfrey give several reasons why Joseph Smith became a Mason on March 15, 1842 and these factors are summarized as follows:

1. Perhaps because of his recent suffering and imprisonment in Missouri, Joseph Smith wanted to secure friendship, acceptance and protection.

2. Since many leading politicians in Illinois were Masons, the Prophet wanted to gain their support and cooperation.

3. Joseph Smith felt comfortable with Masons because some leading members of the Church belonged to that organization: his brother Hyrum, Heber C. Kimball, John C. Bennett, Newell K. Whitney, James Adams, and the prophet's uncle John Smith.

4. Illinois Masons, especially Grand Master Abraham Jonas and Deputy Grand Master James Adams (a Latter-day Saint) wanted LDS loyalty and persuaded Joseph Smith and other Mormons to form a Nauvoo lodge to further Jonas' political ambitions. All political factions in Illinois courted favor with Latter-day Saints when they first arrived in hopes of winning their vote.

5. There was an attraction and admiration for Masonry's cultural and moral values and its example of brotherhood.

6. Joseph wanted and needed social interaction, since he was a warm, friendly outgoing person.

7. Enemies persecuted both Mormons and Masons, and these two groups needed each other.

8. Joseph Smith desired to learn all he could about Masonry, recognizing some similarities between Mormons and Masonry. This point relates to the Masonic belief that they began during the building of Solomon's temple and some claim it goes back to the days of Adam.

Further Reading: EM (1992), 2:527–529.

8.13. Since the Bible is against secrecy, are LDS temple activities in violation of this concept?

Some wrongly use scriptures to prove Christ was against secrecy, pointing out the Savior taught "in secret have I said nothing" (John 18:20). In context the Lord also said "Why asketh thou me? ask them which heard me," as if to say, I do not need to testify against myself; the burden of proof is on you. Christ made this clear when He added, "If I have spoken evil, bear witness of the evil" (John 18:21–23). When Christ said, "For nothing is secret, that shall not be made manifest" (Luke 8:16–17), He was talking not about secret ideas, but about proclaiming the truthfulness and foundations of the gospel. He wants His followers to let their good works shine forth for all to see.

The Bible often speaks of hidden or secret knowledge. Amos stated, "Surely the Lord God will do nothing, but he revealeth his *secret* unto his servants the prophets" (Amos 3:7; emphasis added). After coming down from the Mount of Transfiguration, Christ told Peter, James, and John: "Tell the vision to no man . . ." (Matt. 17:9).

The Savior wanted only His closest followers to know certain things He taught. His disciples asked, "Why speakest thou unto them in parables?" He answered them, "Because it is given unto you to know the *mysteries* of the kingdom of heaven, but to them it is not given" (Matt. 13:10–11; emphasis added). Christ also said, "I have yet many things to say unto you, but ye cannot bear them now" (John

16:12). Christ repeated the idea in Mark 4:11 and Luke 8:10. Jesus also "commanded them to tell no man that [he was Christ]" (Luke 9:21).

Paul, writing to the Saints, said, "I would not . . . that ye should be ignorant of this *mystery*" (Rom. 11:25). In the same letter, Paul spoke of the preaching of Jesus Christ, "according the revelation of the *mystery*, which was kept *secret* since the world began" (Rom. 16:25). Paul said, "We speak the wisdom of God in a *mystery*, even the *hidden wisdom*, which God ordained before the world unto our glory" (1 Cor. 2:7). Paul also said "[Let us be] stewards of the *mysteries* of God" (1 Cor. 4:1). "Though I . . . understand all *mysteries*," . . . and have not charity, I am nothing," Paul said (1 Cor. 13:2). "Behold, I shew you a *mystery*," Paul also said in talking about the resurrection (1 Cor. 15:51). "By revelation [God] made known unto me the *mystery*" (Eph. 3:3; emphasis added).

Many more such scriptures are in the Bible. One can easily make a case that there were some in biblical times who had knowledge from God that non-Church members and some members did not yet have.

8.14. Were Old Testament temples no longer needed when Christianity was established?

Since Latter-day Saints are the only ones today who have temples, critics claim they were phased out in Christ's day and only continued for a time. Christ renounced many Jewish traditions, but not the temple, though many were abusing the temple in the Savior's day. Christians and most Jews were not permitted into the inner parts of the temple courts. Only Jewish priests were allowed to go there. However, Christ, Peter, and Paul made visits to the outer courts of the temple often. The Bible's only recorded instance from the Savior's youth was when His parents took Him to the temple.

Driving the money changers from the temple, Jesus said, "make not *my Father's house* an house of merchandise" (John 2:16; emphasis added). Would Christ have (more than once) driven the money changers out of the temple had He not cared for that holy edifice? At times Christ went daily to the temple to teach (see Matt. 26:55). Dozens of New Testament scriptures refer to the temple. After Christ's ascension, the Saints "worshiped him, and returned to Jerusalem with great joy: And were continually in the temple, praising and blessing God" (Luke 24:53).

It is true, the temples of old had some functions different from today. With Christ having fulfilled the "old law" and completed the Atonement by His suffering, new purposes for temples became necessary. For example, Christ's sacrifice eliminated animal sacrifice that was previously used to point to the coming of the Savior. Critics often ignore the prophecy that at the end of the world Christ will come to His temple (Mal. 3:1).

CHAPTER NINE
Historical Concerns

9.1. Are changes in LDS historical texts a problem?

Critics have mistakenly concluded that modification and additions were fabricated afterthoughts. Evidence shows that changes in LDS texts were corrections and refinements or based on new information as it became available. Does anyone ever write and, upon looking at it later, not find a better way to say it? Do not most who write think of additional things they want to add as they fine-tune what they have written?

Joseph Smith did edit earlier accounts of LDS history and added material left out. However, he forthrightly wrote several times in his journal that he was correcting the history. Brigham Young and others who worked on manuscripts after the Prophet's death said the same. These were honest attempts to set the record straight.

Changes are also understandable since Joseph Smith relied heavily on scribes and historians who were sometimes negligent. Some missing documents may yet be found that will complete gaps in LDS history. All histories of nations, including religions and all aspects of the human story, have missing information. New sources and information occasionally come forth about biblical events and texts. Changes made in history (secular or religious) are not necessarily distortions or falsifications. Scholars often update and write new history books based on the latest research. For example, recently published histories about Abraham Lincoln contain previously unknown facts.

Joseph Smith was not always able to be an accurate journal keeper, especially in his early life, and often he did not write anything about some events as they occurred. With all his other priorities, this is understandable. "Those who make history often do not have time to write history" (Reynolds, 1982. 223). All we know about Jesus Christ is what His followers wrote. It is remarkable that the LDS Prophet had as much time as he did to write or dictate to scribes.

Perhaps Joseph Smith was reluctant to publish certain sacred experiences, such as the First Vision, because when he told others, he suffered intense persecution. Later, the Prophet did not feel as restricted in giving a more complete account of his experiences, as the next chapter details.

Further Reading: Reynolds (1982) 221–232.

9.2. Was the Latter-day Saint "United Order" a form of communism?

All communal programs are not communistic. The United Order is an LDS term sometimes used to describe cooperative economic programs of the Church during the early days of Mormonism. Perhaps it is similar to what some biblical Christians practiced when they "had all things common" (Acts 2:44). The plan is quite different from communism, and is not theocratic communism. An alternate LDS term for "United Order" is "Law of Consecration." A few differences between the LDS program and communism follow.

The LDS Law of Consecration	Communism
Individual property ownership is essential	Individual property ownership is discouraged or forbidden
Individuals have a right to discontinue participation	No choice is given to participate
Each person has his/her separate stewardship; surplus production goes into storehouses for the poor and needy	Most or all of production is controlled by the state
Participation requires keeping God's laws	God's laws are not involved
Voting decides the use of surpluses accumulated in the storehouse not needed by the poor	There are no voting rights; five-year quotas are set by state

The LDS Law of Consecration	Communism
Individuals may draw upon the management skills of leadership for personal training and consultation to run a personal stewardship	Leadership determines what a person must do
Personal responsibility is expected	Leadership makes many decisions for society
Existence of God is declared	Operates under a godless philosophy
The organization exists for the benefit of the individual	Individual exists for the benefit of the organization

Early attempts to live the LDS Law of Consecration were met with mixed success. It worked well in Utah settlements, especially before the railroad arrived, while Latter-day Saints lived in isolation. While the Church was still in the east, with much persecution and members forced to flee from place to place, it could not function well. When practiced by righteous, committed participants, the Law of Consecration solves one of mankind's perennial problems—the struggle between the haves and the have nots. LDS members believe the Messiah will reestablish this principle when He returns to earth.

Further Readings: Arrington (1958); *EM* (1992) 1:312; 4:1493.

9.3. Was Joseph Smith's candidacy for the U.S. presidency a plot to take over the country?

It is inconceivable with the United States Constitution guaranteeing a separation of powers in the three branches of government—the executive (the president), the legislative (Congress), and the judiciary (the courts)—that any religious leader could seize control of the nation. With elections every four years and impeachment power resting with Congress, there is further restriction on abuse of presidential power.

Joseph Smith became a third party candidate to allow Latter-day Saints the opportunity to vote for someone not opposed to the Church. The two major political parties had turned against the Mormons and they knew they could not count on help from the federal government. Joseph Smith earlier visited with U.S. President Martin Van Buren and appealed for redress for the wrongs committed against the Latter-day Saints in Missouri. The president replied, "Your cause is just, but I can do nothing for you" (*HC* 4:80). Joseph Smith and his followers were aware that he had no chance of winning, but as a candidate, he had the opportunity to proclaim the LDS side of the false reports that were circulating. The press began to carry stories about Mormonism and the merits of Joseph Smith's political platform to a national audience.

A study of the political proposals advocated by Joseph Smith shows that they were very profound and farsighted. His notion of having the government sell western lands and using the revenue to purchase slaves and set them free could have averted the Civil War. (Abraham Lincoln proposed a similar plan twenty years later as president during the Civil War, but Congress defeated the proposal.) Other ideas such as rehabilitating and training prisoners, and a federal banking system were advanced for the time. The murder of Joseph Smith in 1844 ended his candidacy along with notable ideas the other candidates did not pursue.

Further readings: Smith (1902), 6:187–188; Smith (1963), 356–357.

9.4. Did Joseph Smith claim "to lay a foundation that will revolutionize the world"?

Critics sometimes use this quotation to assert that the LDS Church has plans for militant world domination. However, in context, Joseph Smith also explained, "It will not be by the sword or gun that this kingdom will roll on" (*HC* 6:365). Without the inclusion of this nonviolent statement, the first part alone could be interpreted as militant, but the entire quotation is not. In matters of dispute, the LDS Church advocates working through legal channels "according to the laws and constitution of the people, which I have suffered to be established" (D&C 101:77).

9.5. Why did animosity develop against Latter-day Saints in Nauvoo?

Latter-day Saints fled Missouri in the winter of 1838–39 because of inhumane atrocities committed against them and the governor's extermination order. Most fled to Illinois, where both political parties welcomed them and wanted to win their support. The people of Quincy took pity on the Mormon refugees and were especially kind and rendered much assistance. Illinois leaders, including Abraham Lincoln and Stephen Douglas, granted the Mormons a most liberal charter that gave them broad powers. Latter-day Saints built their city of Nauvoo on the banks of a horseshoe bend of the Mississippi River, eighteen miles north of Keokuk, Iowa. Latter-day Saints who had fled from New York, Ohio, and Missouri were surprised at the generous provisions in the charter. They welcomed an opportunity to have more control of their own community. The Nauvoo Charter allowed them to have their own courts, schools, and a military organization. The Mormon city also had a democratic form of government subject to the laws of Illinois and the United States. These rights were similar to a charter enjoyed by Quincy, Illinois, but not by towns close to Nauvoo. The city blossomed with beautiful brick homes, productive gardens, and industry. Arts and education flourished. This was in sharp contrast to neighboring towns, which had typical primitive frontier environments. The majestic, towering temple began to take shape. (In 2002 the Nauvoo Temple was rebuilt to its original specifications, with some interior changes to reflect today's usage.)

The grandeur, success, and the rapid growth of Nauvoo (an Indian word meaning *beautiful*) increased. Almost daily, converts arrived from other areas of the United States, Canada, and Great Britain, causing jealousy and suspicion in surrounding communities. Nauvoo became the second largest city in Illinois, second only to rapidly growing Chicago. With the beginning practice of plurality of wives more animosity arose. Sometimes the trouble involved disgruntled members of the Church who united with the enemies. (See chapter six, questions 6.5 and 6.6 dealing with plural marriage.) The first peace and prosperity the Latter-day Saints enjoyed since the Church began lasted only five years.

9.6. Was the assassination of Joseph Smith a result of his destroying his critics' press?

Plots against Joseph Smith's life happened before the printing press incident. However, it is true, the Nauvoo City Council (with Joseph Smith as mayor) ordered the press to be destroyed and this emboldened his enemies to bring about his death. The mob set fire to its own building to make the incident look worse. Although the city council's action was a mistake, the events leading up to the incident must be considered. The Latter-day Saint leader was the object of persecution from the beginning of his prophetic career in 1820. He was forced to flee three states, was constantly harassed by baseless lawsuits, and was once imprisoned for six months without a judgment. Yet his history is filled with kindness, forgiveness, and generosity.

The Nauvoo City Council reacted to threats, slander, and libel. On June 7, 1844, the publishers of the *Nauvoo Expositor*, an anti-Mormon newspaper, in its only issue, threatened to destroy the LDS Church and kill Joseph Smith. "Joseph Smith [is] the biggest villain that goes unhung [sic]," the paper contended (Ludlow, 1992, 3:996).

Critics do not mention that the arrest and imprisonment of Joseph Smith were illegal on the part of the state of Illinois. The judge at Carthage (the county seat), with Illinois Governor Thomas Ford standing by, added treason against the state to the original charge of inciting riot. This made the charge a felony instead of a misdemeanor. To take this action without a preliminary hearing was illegal. The accusation was so blatantly outrageous it would surely have been dropped (and the enemies knew it). Now Joseph Smith could be held in Carthage.

When Joseph Smith and his brother Hyrum arrived in Carthage in custody of sixty armed militia, the mobs jeered the Prophet. They planned quick action while Joseph Smith was in the custody of the state, allegedly for protection. Joseph Smith had cooperated and disarmed the Nauvoo state-authorized militia when Governor Ford gave the order. The governor had also promised Joseph Smith safety if he would come to Carthage to stand trial, a promise the governor didn't keep. He also broke his pledge when he returned to Nauvoo without Joseph Smith. Governor Ford also reduced the number of guards who were supposed to be protecting the Prophet in Carthage Jail with full knowledge of an armed mob lurking nearby.

Critics applying of the twentieth century "freedom of press" standards to nineteenth-century frontier America, where vigilante actions were common, was unwarranted, especially when only applied to Mormons. The actions of the Nauvoo City Council were illegal, but they certainly did not warrant a charge of treason and murdering the Latter-day Saint Prophet, who claimed he was innocent and willing to be judged in court. When Joseph left Nauvoo for the last time he said, "I have a conscience void of offense toward God and toward all men" (Smith (1963), 376).

Further Readings: Godfrey (1967); Ludlow (1992), 3:996–997; Oaks and Hill (1979); Oaks (1965), 862–903.

9.7. Since the offshoots of Mormonism each claim to be the true Church, is this a concern?

With the premature death of Joseph Smith and with no established precedent, there was uncertainty among many Latter-day Saints concerning the succession of leadership. The Saints were shocked and caught off guard when their 38-year-old Prophet, who had miraculous escapes all his life, was dead. Although the Doctrine and Covenants gives clear guidelines on succession, most members did not know what they were. All of the Twelve Apostles were away on missions except John Taylor. He was in Nauvoo, severely injured from the wounds he had received when Joseph Smith and Joseph's brother Hyrum were murdered. This dispersion of the Twelve added to the confusion. Within a month they had all returned and a special public meeting was held which resolved the issue that Brigham Young and the Twelve Apostles should now lead the Church. Where priesthood authority resided was the determining factor to answer the question of succession. The following points support The Church of Jesus Christ of Latter-day Saints:

1. LDS scripture affirms God and His Son, Jesus Christ, restored their Church for the last time.

Though some would fall away, the Church would not be discontinued (Dan. 2:44; D&C 13:1; 27:13; 90:2; 1 Ne. 14:1–2).

2. LDS scriptures make it clear that leadership in the

Church requires three conditions.

A. a person must be called by one having authority

B. a person has to be ordained by one having authority

C. a person called to a position of leadership must be presented to the appropriate congregation for a sustaining vote. A higher authorized leader must conduct this procedure also called common consent (D&C 26; 41:9; 42:11). This vital provision keeps deception from creeping into the Church. This third requirement is especially important since many offshoots of Mormonism trace their authority to a person who they claim secretly received it many years ago.

3. Before the prophet's death he bestowed all "Keys of Authority" upon the Twelve Apostles.

Although apostles and other in the Church hold the Melchizedek Priesthood offices, permission to exercise leadership must also include receiving a conferral of that permission from a higher authority. This permission to lead is known as Keys of the Priesthood (see Ludlow, 1992) 3:1420; 4:1640; Esplin, 1981, 319–320). This procedure is similar to a person who is sworn in as a soldier in an army, but who must wait for his official orders from higher officers telling him when and where to serve. Latter-day Saint scripture states that the quorum of Twelve Apostles holds equal authority with the First Presidency of the Church (see D&C 107:22–24). When all the apostles were back in Nauvoo, they found that several members claimed they were the rightful heirs to lead the Church. At the special meeting called by Brigham Young, he reminded the Saints that the Twelve had received all Keys of the Priesthood from Joseph Smith and they should lead the Church. Next he asked for a sustaining vote from the congregation, which was unanimous. Thus, Brigham Young followed the principles of delegated authority and common consent necessary to lead in the Church as previously explained.

4. A spiritual manifestation supports Brigham Young's succession.

A remarkable supernatural phenomenon took place when Brigham Young, the senior ranking apostle, addressed the Church at a public meeting. Several in the audience recorded in their journals that Brigham Young sounded and looked like Joseph Smith on that occasion (see Smith (1963), 388). Apparently the Lord caused this miracle to make sure His people followed the principles of succession given in the Doctrine and Covenants.

5. Brigham Young's leadership was prophesied.

Joseph Smith, upon meeting Brigham Young for the first time, said he would one day preside over the Church. This was in September 1832 (see Roberts (1930), 1:289). Before Joseph's death, Brigham was only one of two of the original Twelve still alive who had never turned against the Prophet. The other was Heber C. Kimball, who became President Young's first counselor in the First Presidency.

6. The LDS Church's validity is supported by the Rocky Mountain Prophecy.

Joseph Smith in 1842 prophesied that the Saints would soon be in the Rocky Mountains. This declaration gives support to Brigham Young as the legitimate successor to Joseph Smith. In 1844, he also prophesied this would happen within five years (see question 9.15). That the vast majority of the Latter-day Saints in the United States and abroad followed Brigham Young in the exodus to Utah gives further support to LDS claims.

7. The continuation of temples identifies the legitimate Church.

The continuation of one of the main fundamentals of the restoration, temple building and the essential ordinances performed therein, is only done by The Church of Jesus Christ of Latter-day Saints.

Further Readings: Durham and Heath (1970); Ludlow (1992), 3:1421–1422).

CHAPTER TEN
Prophecies Examined

10.1. If a prophet makes a false prophecy or statement, is he still a prophet?

Only one perfect person ever lived—Jesus Christ. Prophets can err, but that does not diminish their prophetic calling. Speaking through the prophet Moses, God said: "When a prophet speaketh in the name of the Lord, if the thing follow not, nor come to pass, that is the thing which the Lord hath not spoken, but the prophet hath spoken it presumptuously" (Deut. 18:22). This makes clear that prophets are not always correct. The Lord did not say that such an occurrence makes the prophet false, only presumptuous. This agrees with the statement made by Joseph Smith: "I told them that a prophet was a prophet only when he was acting as such" (*HC*, 5:265).

Notice, the scripture said, "*When* a prophet speaketh in the name of the Lord. . . ." (emphasis added). This certainly means a prophet may also speak when it is not in the name of the Lord. If this were not true, a prophet could never utter a word unless he has a direct revelation from God. Neither Joseph Smith, the LDS Church, any prophet in the LDS Church, nor any biblical prophet, has claimed perfection for prophets. In a general conference, J. Reuben Clark, Jr., a member of the First Presidency said that the First Presidency is "not infallible in our judgment, and we err" (in Conference Report, Apr. 1940, 14). Church President Spencer W. Kimball has likewise said "I make no claim of infallibility" (in Conference Report, April 1970, 120).

One of the foremost Protestant biblical commentators has commented about prophets.

> Though purified and ennobled by the influence of His Holy Spirit, these men each had his own peculiarities of manner and disposition—each with his own education or want of education—each with his own way of looking at things—each influenced differently from one another by the different experiences and disciplines of his life. Their inspiration did not involve a suspension of the natural faculties; it did not even make them free from earthly passions; it did not make them into machines—it left them men. . . . Therefore we find their knowledge sometimes no higher than that of their contemporaries (Dummelow cxxxv).

Critics of the Church seize upon every word that has been "spoken" by LDS leaders and try to find fault. Although a certain prophecy may seem false, there may be other explanations:

1. The statement in question does not come from a primary source.

2. The source may not have been reported correctly.

3. The prophecy may have been conditional, such as when the Lord told Jonah that Nineveh would be destroyed if the people did not repent. The inhabitants repented and the city was not destroyed.

4. A prophecy may have an entirely different meaning when taken in its full context.

5. A particular prophecy may yet have future fulfillment.

We must not lose sight of the fact that a prophet's primary role is to call people to repentance and urge them to live moral lives. Prophesying has always been a minor function of a prophet.

Further Readings: McConkie (1998) 50; McConkie (1966) 544–547.

10.2. Are Latter-day Saints wrong quoting the "Civil War" prophecy to extol Joseph Smith?

A prophecy given by Joseph Smith in December 1837 stated that a civil war in the United States would begin with a rebellion at South Carolina (see D&C 87). The first reason some belittle this prophecy is that newspapers of the day reported an actual rebellion brewing at that very time at Fort Sumter, South Carolina. Since the rebellion ended quietly a few months later, it looked like the prophecy would never be fulfilled.

The Prophet Joseph Smith stuck by his prediction when he repeated it in an 1843 revelation, stating that the Lord had told him the war would begin in South Carolina (D&C 130:12–13). When Civil War began in the United States in 1861, it was at Fort Sumter, South Carolina. By the year 1851, Latter-day Saints had published the 1832 prophecy in English as part of a missionary handbook called the Pearl of Great Price. In 1880, the Church canonized it in the Pearl of Great Price, which became the fourth volume of LDS scripture. Later, Church leaders switched the prophecy to the Doctrine and Covenants as Section 87.

10.3. Did the "Zion's Camp" revelation fail with the LDS surrender to Missouri forces?

In 1833, mobs forced Latter-day Saints from their homes in Jackson County, Missouri. As a result, the governor, Daniel Dunklin, felt he could not enforce the legal rights of the Mormons, so he suggested that the Latter-day Saints bring an armed contingent from their headquarters in Ohio in order to help the state militia retrieve LDS property (*HC,* 1902, 1:445; see D&C 103). The governor realized he could not maintain his meager state troops indefinitely to guard the homes of private citizens. He suggested to the Saints that with a strong LDS military presence, together with the Missouri militia, the abuse against Mormons might subside. (The action might be compared to sending troops as peacekeepers to trouble spots in the world today.)

However, by the time Zion's Camp arrived in Missouri, rumors and fears of the advancing LDS army caused the non-LDS citizens much concern. No Missouri militia was involved at this point. They formed their own citizen armies to repel the arrival of Zion's Camp. This included burning the abandoned homes of Latter-day Saints in Jackson County and harassing Latter-day Saints who fled to northern Missouri. As the LDS forces marched into Missouri in the summer of 1834 near Richmond, the citizen army approached them at the Fishing River. Five men entered Zion's camp, warning the Mormons that they would be utterly destroyed. Within an hour, a huge hailstorm burst forth, winds uprooted trees, and the river became a raging torrent, dispersing the mobs. The storm did not touch nearby Zion's Camp.

With Missouri on the verge of its own civil war and a national civil war threatening, Governor Dunklin decided not to take sides and join state forces with an LDS army. Joseph Smith at this point decided to negotiate a settlement rather than force a military solution. Although Zion's Camp was prepared to fight if necessary, the intent of the group was to keep the peace and allow Church members the right to occupy their property from which they had been evicted by mob violence.

Some ask why the Lord would call "Zion's Camp" to arms when it failed. The purpose was a nonviolent peacekeeping force, not military aggression. Since the Missouri governor, out of expediency, felt he could not keep his part of the original offer, it is not realistic to expect Latter-day Saints to forge ahead violently into a situation of needless bloodshed, which would have given their enemies excuse to call the Latter-day Saints aggressors. Apparently the Lord also felt the Saints were not yet worthy to redeem the lands (D&C 105:10–14).

With hindsight one can see why the Lord commanded the march. A few in Zion's Camp became disillusioned and left the Church. Most of the camp, who had a deep conviction of Joseph Smith's prophetic calling, came out stronger members as a result of the day-after-day close encounter with their Prophet on a journey that lasted ten weeks and covered nearly a thousand miles.

Many of the future LDS leaders came from this camp. Little did any of the Saints realize that this march was a "dry run" for a much greater trek. A dozen years later, in 1846, many of these same Zion's Camp members would be the leaders of one of the largest mass exoduses in the history of world. Jedediah M. Grant, Orson Hyde, Heber C. Kimball, Orson and Parley P. Pratt, George A. Smith, Wilford Woodruff, Charles C. Rich, and Brigham Young became leaders of the Mormon pioneer trek to Utah.

Further Reading: Smith (1963) 170–177.

10.4. Was the temple in Independence, Missouri to be built during Joseph Smith's lifetime?

The Lord did direct the LDS Prophet to start this temple, but the author is not aware that Joseph Smith claimed he would live to see it completed. Just as the biblical Jews lost their temple on two occasions and still have not realized their dream of rebuilding it in our day, so Latter-day Saints await a temple(s) in Independence. However, the St. Louis temple dedicated in 1997 is certainly an important milestone in LDS history.

One of the revelations in connection with the Independence Temple even states that "after much tribulation come the blessings." Only then might those living in Missouri "be honored in laying the foundation [of the temple]" (D&C 58:7). The revelation never gives a promise that the Mormons in Missouri will see the Temple completed at the time. Soon after the foundation for the Temple was started, the Mormons were forced to flee.

10.5. Did LDS leaders claim that the return to Missouri would happen in "this generation"?

Latter-day Saints often use the word "generation" as did Peter when he said to the Saints in his day, "Ye are a chosen generation" (1 Pet. 2:9). In context, "generation" in this case is broader than a span of one lifetime. Other biblical translations use the word "people" or "nation" instead of "generation" (*American Standard Version* and *New English Bible* are two examples). LDS apostle George A. Smith may have had this broader future concept of "generation" in mind when he said, "Who is there that is prepared for this movement back to the center stake of Zion, and where are the architects amongst us that are qualified to erect this temple and the city that will surround it? We have to learn a great many things, in my opinion, before we are prepared to return to that holy land" (*JD,* 9:71).

Scholar Daniel H. Ludlow has written: "'Generation' may refer to a state or condition as well as to a time period." The dictionary lists several accepted definitions of the word in addition to the commonly accepted 'average span of time between the

214

birth of parents and that of their offspring.' The scriptures refer to an 'unbelieving and stiffnecked generation' (D&C 5:8) and a 'crooked and perverse generation' (D&C 34:6). The Savior said: "An evil and adulterous generation seeketh after a sign" (Matt. 12:39). The Lord is not making reference to a period of years, but to a period of wickedness. All of the foregoing uses of the word "generation" suggest a state or condition rather than a specific period of time. Thus, when the Lord states that a certain thing will occur in 'this generation,' He may be referring to the conditions which are then existing, to a general period of time similar to 'this dispensation'" (Ludlow, 1978, 114).

10.6. Did Brigham Young really want to build the Salt Lake Temple out of sandstone?

Statements are not prophecy, but we will comment anyway. Stone suitable for building a temple in Salt Lake was first thought to be two hundred miles away, and to bring such huge boulders that far in fragile wagons without established roads was prohibitive. Brigham Young was not a geologist, so his theory that sandstone would harden over time was wrong. Adobe was also considered. When large amounts of granite were found in nearby Big Cottonwood Canyon, and when some of the scientists in the LDS Church talked to Brigham Young about the nature of stone, he was easily persuaded to change his mind.

10.7. Did Joseph Smith falsely predict the downfall of the United States?

Joseph Smith said in May 1843, "I prophesy in the name of the Lord God of Israel, unless the United States redress the wrongs committed by her officers that in a few years the government will be utterly overthrown and wasted, and there will not be so much as a potsherd left." Part of this statement to Steven A. Douglas was completely fulfilled when Joseph Smith prophesied his political downfall if he turned against the Latter-day Saints.

Further reading: Smith (1902) 394–398.

10.8. Do LDS people believe the Constitution will "hang by a thread" and the Saints save it?

No such statement in the handwriting of Joseph Smith or one of his scribes exists that this author is aware of. However, several individuals, including Brigham Young, said they heard Joseph Smith state words to that effect. In 1986, LDS President Ezra Taft Benson quoted the Joseph Smith statement and felt that the time would come when "the nation shall lean upon Latter-day Saints and *others* besides LDS people . . . "I have faith that the Constitution will be saved as prophesied by Joseph Smith. But it will not be saved in Washington. The *citizens of this nation* will save it, who love and cherish freedom" (Benson, 1986; emphasis added).

Some maintain that the remarks by Joseph Smith indicate there is an LDS conspiracy to take over the United States. There is no substance or evidence that the LDS Church has intentions to take over political power of the United States. When Jesus Christ's Second Coming occurs, He will reign over the earth as King of kings (see Isaiah 9:6). The Church of Jesus Christ of Latter-day Saints is preparing a people for this event and believes it will be involved in Christ's Kingdom.

Further Readings: Stewart (1976), 64–65; Jessee (1979), 390–391.

10.9. Did Joseph Smith prophesy that the Second Coming of Christ would happen by 1890?

In a revelation in the Doctrine and Covenants, the Lord tells the Prophet, "Joseph, my son, if thou livest until thou art eighty-five years old, thou shalt see the face of the Son of Man; therefore let this suffice and trouble me no more on this matter." Since Joseph Smith would have been eighty-five in 1890, critics claim this is a false revelation. However, the next verse states "I was left thus, without being able to decide whether this coming referred to the beginning of the millennium or to some previous appearing, or whether I should die and thus see his face"

(D&C 130:15–16). Although some Latter-day Saints living before 1890 felt the Second Coming would happen in 1890, in hindsight, it must mean some time following that date.

10.10. When do Latter-day Saints expect Christ's Second Coming to happen?

The official position of the LDS Church is found in Matthew 24:36, which states that "that day and hour knoweth no man, no, not the angels of heaven, but my Father only."

Further Readings: Ludlow (1992) 2:737–739; Lund (1971).

CHAPTER ELEVEN
The Church in Action

It is hoped that faithful members of the LDS Church reading this far have gained information helpful to give answers to family and friends who have concerns about the church or are "blinded by the craftiness of men" (D&C 76:75). Other readers—LDS and non-LDS—are invited to study, ponder and pray to receive a personal witness from God that The Church of Jesus Christ of Latter-day Saints is His restored Church on earth (Moroni 10:3–4). This final chapter differs from most of the controversial previous questions and shows some of the strengths of The Church of Jesus Christ of Latter-day Saints and its people.

11.1. What is the impact of The Church of Jesus Christ of Latter-day Saints on its members?

Research showing the effects of Mormonism on individuals, although once scarce, are becoming more common in professional publications in and out of the Church. As LDS success increases, curiosity

increases among non-LDS scholars in regards to the
Church's principles and people. Some of the following statistics include all Utah people, and will be
identified as such when they do. People from, other
churches, atheists, agnostics and others also affect the
Utah profile. However, the LDS members, that com-
prise about 70% of the state certainly impact Utah's
statistics to a great extent.

1. Church Participation
    "Mormon adults attend church services
    more frequently than U.S. adults overall
    and more often than members of any major
    denominational group." Other surveys sup-
    port this finding (Duke, 1998, 160). In
    America Jesus taught, "Ye shall meet togeth-
    er oft" (3 Nephi 18:22).

2. Chastity
    Comparative studies of adolescents show
    that the LDS emphasis on the biblical prin-
    ciple of chastity results in a much lower rate
    of pre-marital sexual experience than non
    member young people (Duke, 1998, p. 3).
    "I, the Lord God, delight in . . . chastity . . .
    and whoredoms are an abomination" (Jacob
    2:28).

3. Abstinence of Drugs, Alcohol and Tobacco
   Considering the large percentage of Latter-day Saints in Utah, it is not surprising that the state's consumption of tobacco is the lowest in the nation. 50.1 percent of high school seniors in the nation have ever smoked cigarettes, compared with 33.8 percent of Utah students. "Tobacco is not for the body" (D&C 89:8). The same ratios apply to the use of various drugs (Martin, Heaton, Bahr, 1986, 245–257). "[Your bodies] are the temple of God" (1 Cor. 3:16).

   One study showed 27.4 percent of Utahns consumed alcoholic beverages in the previous month, roughly half the national rate of 51.2 percent. Utah ranks last among the fifty states in gallons of alcohol consumed annually per person, sixteen years and over. Utahns consume 21.47 gallons per-capita, compared with 52.00 gallons in New Hampshire and 60.69 gallons in Nevada (Martin, Heaton, Bahr, 1986, 245–257). "Drink not wine nor strong drink" (Judges 13:4). A 1994 study by Stephen J. Bahr and Anastasios C. Marcos states that 80.4 percent of U.S. high school seniors have consumed alcohol in their lives,

GILBERT SCHARFFS

compared with 44.8 percent of Utah seniors. "Strong drinks are not for the belly"
(D&C 89:7).

4. Longevity of Life
    Two exhaustive studies in California, by
    James Enstrom, focusing on active Latter-
    day Saint men and their wives covering a
    period from 1979 to 1993, show that they
    have a life expectancy eight to eleven years
    longer than U.S. whites as a whole.
    Members of the Church had far less cancer
    of all types, far fewer cardiovascular diseases
    and much less of most other diseases (Duke,
    1998, 425–471). Members, because of their
    lifestyle, often obtain preferred rates buying
    insurance. Utah's death rate in 1996 per
    1,000 population was 5.5, the second lowest
    in the United States, and lowest in the west-
    ern states. The average U.S. rate is 8.8. In the
    fifth of the Ten Commandments the Lord
    commands us to so live that our "days may
    be long upon the land" (Exodus 20:12).

    In 1862, Mark Twain, who was not yet
    famous, came through the Salt Lake valley
    collecting material for later books. One of
    his accounts in *Roughing It* was actually
    complimentary. "Salt Lake City was

222

healthy—an extremely healthy city. They declared there was only one physician in the place and he was arrested every week regularly to answer under the vagrant act for having 'no visible means of support.'" (Ayres (1987), 286).

5. Mental Health
    Sociologist Daniel K. Judd studied all the literature on religion and mental well-being that he could find over a ten-year period. He found that eighty-five of the outcomes reviewed "between 1985-1995 indicated either a positive (59 percent) or a neutral (26 percent) relationship between religiosity and mental health" (Duke (1998), 477).

    The same research found fifty-five studies that dealt with LDS people. Although religiosity has benefits for people of most religions, the effects for Latter-day Saints was much higher in most categories (Duke, 479–491). "Be renewed in the spirit of your mind" (Eph. 4:23).

6. Marriage
    Latter-day Saints are more likely than other groups to marry and they are less likely to divorce. The 1990 U.S. census reveals that

nearly 50 percent of U.S. men, ages 25–29, were not married, while this was true of only 30 percent of comparable Utah men. For women in this age group two-thirds had not married for the nation at large, while less that half of Utah women had not done so (Heaton, Hirschl, Chadwick, 1998, 93). "The Lord God said, It is not good that the man should be alone" (Gen. 2:18). "Let every man have his own wife, and let every wife have her own husband. Let the husband render unto the wife due benevolence: and likewise also the wife unto the husband" (1 Cor. 7:2–3). "Marriage is ordained of God" (D&C 49:15).

One study shows that more Latter-day Saints over age thirty are married or have been married than any other group. LDS people in that group had far fewer divorces than other groups. (Duke, 1998, 276). For Latter-day Saints, depending on which study, who get married in the temple the divorce rate ranges from 1/10 to 1/5 of members who do not marry in the temple "What therefore God hath joined together, let not man put asunder" (Mark 10:9).

7. Contentment in Marriage
    Kenneth R. Smith and Julie K. Shipman
    studied marital happiness in Utah in 1990.
    They asked married couples to rate their
    happiness on a scale of one to seven with
    seven being the highest. "For married cou-
    ples aged 18–44, whose youngest child is
    under age five, we find that marital happi-
    ness is high with most near six on the seven-
    point scale. . . . Active Mormons report
    higher levels of happiness than other
    Utahns" (Heaton, Hirschl, Chadwick,
    1998, 101). "Neither is the man without
    the woman, neither the woman without the
    man in the Lord" (1 Cor. 11:11).

8. Happiness
    A study comparing Latter-day Saints with
    national samples, concluded that "Mormon
    respondents have a higher level of overall
    happiness than the American populace"
    (Duke, 1998, 490). Within the LDS sample
    it showed that the greater the commitment
    to the teachings of the Church, the greater
    the happiness. Joseph Smith taught "happi-
    ness is the object of our existence" and the
    Book of Mormon declared, "Men are that
    they might have joy" (2 Ne. 2:25).

9. Two-parent Families
Abundant research supports that a two-parent family produces fewer children with social problems—fewer juvenile arrests, fewer school dropouts and higher income. Thomas A. Hirschl points out that 83 percent of Utah children belong to "married couple families compared with the national average of 70 percent. Only 12 percent of Utah children belong to single-parent families compared with 20 percent for the nation" (Heaton, Hirschl, Chadwick, 1996, 234).

10. Decent Adolescent Behavior
Skeptics have generally thought that in society as a whole religiosity plays no role on delinquent behavior. A study by Bruce A. Chadwick and Brent L. Top found that peers, family *and* religion all have influence on young people. These researchers have concluded that LDS youths who internalize religious values and beliefs and engage in religious practices are seldom involved in delinquent activities (Duke, 1998, 518). Thus we see that faithful parents and the Church are likely to have a good influence on their children even when positive peer

group influence is lacking or small. "Teach [God's word] diligently to thy children" Deut. 7:6).

11. Conviction, Yet Tolerance
Latter-day Saints are 85 percent "more likely to believe that their Church is the true church compared with other denominations that ranged from 2 percent to 23 percent." Some might conclude, this makes Latter-day Saints less tolerant. This study also found 78 percent of LDS people felt others should have the right to worship as they pleased if they did not infringe upon others. Other denominations ranged from only 39 percent to 50 percent (Duke, 1998, 92). "Therefore, O ye that embark in the service of God, see that ye serve him with all your heart, might, mind and strength" (D&C 4:2). LDS theology also encompasses the belief that there is much good and many righteous people in other religions. The eleventh article of faith requires LDS members to accept all people worshiping how, when, or what they may. "All men are privileged the one like unto the other" (2 Nephi 26:28).

12. Education

    Since Utah ranks lowest in dollars spent per student per capita some conclude that the state must not value education. Utah has the highest birth rate and largest population between grades kindergarten and twelve, which is why the state spends less per pupil than any state in the Union. Usually ignored is the fact that for every $1,000 Utahns earn, 9.2 percent goes to pay for education, which is highest in the nation. This is even more remarkable since Utah is the sixteenth highest taxing state in the country (*Money Magazine,* January 1994). In education Utah always ranks at or near the top in number of high school and college graduates. "To be learned is good if they hearken to the counsels of God" (2 Ne. 9:29).

13. Self Sufficiency

    Utah's poverty rate was the nation's second lowest in 1998, 8.4 percent, barely behind New Hampshire with 8.3 percent. The United States poverty average for 1998 was 13.25 percent or 56 percent higher than Utah's rate (*Deseret News,* 2 Oct. 1999, sec. B, p.1). Utah's unemployment rate in the

1990s was usually about 1 percent lower than the national average. Utah ranks first in home ownership. There are great efforts made by the church members to help through generous payment of tithes and fast offerings, but also by encouraging people to help themselves. "Wo unto you rich men that will not give your substance to the poor" (D&C 56:16).

11.2. Why is the LDS Church Welfare Plan so successful and how is it seen by others?

The Heritage Foundation, a Washington, D.C. think-tank, in its journal *Policy Review*, published an article by their assistant editor, Tucker Carlson, which was carried internationally by the Associated Press: "Their welfare system provides material necessities while focusing on strengthening the family, teaching a vigorous work ethic and helping the needy help themselves." He said other would do well to study the LDS program. Mormons realize that welfare "has the same properties as nitroglycerine: If used correctly, it can heal and sustain; if used wantonly, it will certainly destroy." Carlson continued, "A sign of the system's success is that able-bodied people on it become independent on an average of about 100 days. Compare this with the federal welfare system in which half of the families . . . will remain on the dole for more than ten years." (Recent government regulations limit welfare payments for those able to work to four years.)

Carlson outlined several more reasons he found why the [LDS] system is highly successful and why government welfare is not: 1) Mormon welfare recipients work for what they receive. 2) Home teachers visit church members each month and report to local leaders the needs of members. 3) Unpaid local bishops, who are often professionals or business owners, administer the system. Bishops tailor benefits to exact needs and no more, opting to pay bills and give food instead of cash. 5) Leaders teach members to budget, live on their incomes and provide training to make beneficiaries self sufficient. 6) Before they give help to needy members, the Church urges children and other family members to provide as much assistance as they can (*Salt Lake Tribune,* 15 February 1992, 1).

Latter-day Saints realize the main reason for the success of its welfare program is that it came through revelation from the Lord. LDS president Heber J. Grant stated in 1936, when the Church started the current welfare system, "Our purpose is to help people help themselves."

In 1997, Elder Thomas S. Monson of the Church's First Presidency reviewed LDS welfare programs at an annual Rotary International banquet. These include "100 supermarket-style storehouses, eighty canneries, ninety-seven employment centers worldwide, forty-five Deseret Industry stores, fifty-three local LDS Social Services, and 4,800 welfare missionaries in thirty-three countries" (*Deseret News* 21 November 1997, sec. A, p.1).

Many non-Latter-day Saints recognize that the LDS welfare program is the most successful in the world. Visitors to any of the LDS global storehouse and welfare centers are impressed. Author Glen L. Rudd, in his book *Pure Religion,* gives examples of responses received from those who have toured Welfare Square in Salt Lake City.

A Baptist from Texas wrote, "A true picture of pure Christianity." A Jewish visitor from Israel said: "Never before have I felt the spirit of the Bible so alive as within the LDS Church." From Colorado two Congregationalists stated, "This is one of the most unforgettable experiences we have had in a long time. Only divine guidance could have formed such an organization." A Catholic (no address given) said: "God has his eyes on this organization. May its members continue to live this way. It is uplifting to see that people can still work together." A Presbyterian from New Jersey commented, "The work done here should be universal and until we do it, there will be no hope for peace." A Christian from Missouri asserted, "The most wonderful place I have ever been" (Excerpts from Rudd (1995), 191–200).

What impresses most visitors is the look of

accomplishment on the faces of the many handi-
capped workers. Were it not for this opportunity to
clean, mend, restore, and repair broken items that
have been donated, they would not have employment
that provides a living wage. This recycling of goods in
a throw-away society also helps the environment.
However, most of the work rendered is by volunteers
and those working in exchange for assistance received.

Reverend Norman Vincent Peale, of New York
City's famous Marble Collegiate Church, spent two
hours at Welfare Square in Salt Lake City in 1975,
and said, "Here is one of the greatest demonstrations
of practical Christianity I have ever seen."

President Ronald Reagan at a White House break-
fast with leaders gathered to discuss welfare initiatives
introduced Thomas Monson of the LDS First
Presidency to the group. He "represents an organization
that truly knows how to care for its own." President
Reagan then described aspects of the LDS program and
his visit to the LDS welfare cannery in Sacramento,
California, while he was governor. Along with other
White House officials, President Reagan visited the
facilities in Ogden, Utah, and again gave high praise.

11.3. Besides caring for its own, how does the LDS Church welfare program benefit others?

In the speech to Rotarians, Elder Monson mentioned some of the humanitarian relief given by the

Latter-day Saints in recent years. "Church members from the United States and Canada participated in two special fasts that provided $11 million for aid to the people of Ethiopia, Chad, and other sub-Saharan Nations during the 1985 famine." In 1996, suffering populations around the world received church aid that included sufficient clothing to outfit 8.7 million people in 58 countries. More than one million pounds of medical and educational equipment were sent to seventy countries" (*Deseret News*, 21 Nov. 1997).

It is amazing that every day about 12 tons of clothing, from what is called the Salt Lake sort center, goes to needy areas around the world. Also sent are medical supplies, text books and educational material. Similar centers exist around the world, and where Church membership is small, the collecting and sorting take place by volunteers in member homes.

In 1945, after World War II, the LDS Church sent relief supplies to Europe. This was one year before the United States announced its Marshall Plan to help rebuild Europe. By 1949, they had sent the equivalent of 140 boxcar loads, including much aid to former enemies. The LDS Church gave supplies to the German government, the Lutheran and Catholic churches for distribution, as well as to its own members.

Holland was occupied by the hated Nazis during the war. However, when hostilities ceased, the Dutch Latter-day Saints, hearing the plight of the Germans was worse than their own suffering, sent much of their own potato welfare harvest to the suffering Germans. One Dutch widow refused to accept her allotment saying, "If others are giving theirs, I want my potatoes to go to the Germans, too" (Scharffs, 1970, 57–59).

At 11:57 A.M., Saturday, June 5, 1976, the 307-foot-high Teton Dam in southeastern Idaho collapsed, unleashing eighty billion gallons in a wall of water fifty feet high on homes and farmland. The flood virtually destroyed several communities with eleven lives lost, 4,000 injured, 2,000 left homeless. The damages covered more than three hundred square miles. The destruction amounted to more than one billion dollars. Within hours the Church in Utah supplemented the relief efforts of local civic and other relief organizations. In Salt Lake City, 150 miles away, a tractor-trailer rig was loaded and on its way north to Rexburg by 5:00 P.M. It arrived before nightfall with food and sleeping supplies for the homeless. Other trucks soon arrived from LDS welfare facilities in Idaho.

The Church's Ricks College, on a hill in Rexburg, escaped the flood and was used to care for most of the victims in its cafeterias and student dormitories. Fortunately, school had ended a few days earlier and most students had left town. In the first week after the flood, 14,000 Latter-day Saint volun-

teers arrived including 450 licensed electricians, to
begin the cleanup and rebuilding. A church leader in
Soda Springs, Idaho, 165 miles away, arranged to
send 150 tractors and front-end loaders. "Estimated
time donated by volunteer Church members exceed-
ed one million man hours" (Rudd, 1995, 261–267).

"In the 1980s, severe drought caused great suffering to millions of people in Africa. In 1985, the
Church held two special fast days. . . . [Members]
freely gave nearly eleven million dollars. A large
amount of this money went to help the people of
Kenya." The Church joined forces with other relief
agencies building portable water systems. One
woman said when she turned on the first spigot of
pure water in her home, "For the past 40 years, I have
walked eight miles each way every day to get water for
my family. . . . This is like a dream." Some 1,100
other dwellings in the area received clean water.
Today, the Church extends such projects to other
countries (Rudd, 1995, 267–268).

In February 1990, Hurricane Ofa struck the
islands of Western Samoa, American Samoa and
other islands. Winds more than 200 miles an hour
destroyed approximately 2,200 homes. Twenty
months later Hurricane Val hit the same vicinity.
Each time the Latter-day Saints sent relief from
Australia, New Zealand, Hawaii, and the U.S. main-
land (Rudd, 1995, 268–272).

Hurricane Andrew struck the southern part of Florida in 1992, the worst natural disaster in U.S. history in terms of property damage. Before Andrew reached the coast, the Church moved its spearhead unit from Atlanta, Georgia, to Orlando, Florida, to wait until it became clear where the storm would strike. . . . The hurricane damaged one hundred and sixty square miles of Miami and devastated or severely damaged eighty-five thousand houses leaving more than 225,000 people homeless . . . [including] more than 1,000 members of the South Miami Florida Stake.

On the day after the storm, Latter-day Saints began arriving from all over the southeast area of the United States. "Eighteen hundred volunteers came to help on the first weekend, 5,100 helped on the Labor Day weekend." A non-LDS helicopter pilot flew President George Bush and the two other presidential candidates, Bill Clinton and Ross Perot, over the destruction area. They asked about the many volunteers on the ground wearing yellow T-shirts? The pilot replied, "Those are my friends, Mormon volunteer rescue workers." Responses from the three dignitaries included, "Wonderful," "Marvelous," and "God bless the Mormons." A summary of the accomplishments included temporary roofs and windows on some 3,000 structures including "a Jewish synagogue and three Christian chapels. The volunteers removed tons of debris and brought ten trailer loads of food, water, emergency medical supplies" (Rudd, 1995, 272–275).

In the Northridge area of southern California an earthquake measuring 6.6 on the Richter scale caused extreme devastation in January 1994, killing 54 people and causing an estimated $15 billion in damages. Latter-day Saints set up three tent cities furnishing food and shelter for several hundred people. When supplies ran out, "members in the Los Angeles area collected funds to purchase additional food, medical, hygienic, and baby supplies and furnished blankets and coats. [LDS youth groups also] brought candy and balloons for children and organized games for them. "Stake leaders asked members to provide food for a Catholic relief agency to distribute. Other members outside the Los Angeles Basin collected fifteen tons of food and supplies, which they delivered to a Methodist church that served as the distribution center. The Church provided relief supplies to the Salvation Army for meals in a Los Angeles park" (Rudd, 1995, pp. 276-277).

Floods in southern Georgia caused by tropical storm Alberto brought 23 inches of continuous rain during a 24-hour period in 1994. Thirty-five thousand families were evacuated. "The American Red Cross used two Latter-day Saint chapels [as shelters] . . . Within five hours of requested help, spearhead units dispatched from the Atlanta [LDS] welfare complex arrived with the first supplies. . . . This shipment included fresh water, food, medical supplies, shovels, wheelbarrows, axes, saws, generators, water coolers, ladders and many other items. The Church provided nine 18-wheel truckloads of supplies and more than six thousand LDS volunteers rotated working during the next three weekends" (Rudd, 1995, 277–279).

The Red Cross, many public, private and church agencies do much to alleviate suffering around the globe. Latter-day Saints are part of these noble efforts. Other churches, which alleviate suffering, such as Catholic Charities receive LDS funds and supplies because, in some situations, they have better distribution capabilities. Latter-day Saints accept ongoing assignments to help in the Catholic-operated St. Vincent de Paul soup kitchen in Salt Lake City.

President Monson concluded his report to the Rotarians: "I often [ask the question] 'Do we have responsibility to do something about the terrible suffering worldwide?' Yes, we are our brothers' keepers . . . The church has donated $3.1 million worth of food, medical supplies . . . to alleviate suffering and starvation in North Korea. Ships at sea right now are taking more food to the children, primarily in North Korea, he said. Hunger knows no ecclesiastical boundaries. We can provide hope. We can provide life" (*Deseret News*, 21 Nov. 1997, sec. A, p.1).

When floods hit Salt Lake City in June 1983, Mayor Ted Wilson acted fast. He called LDS leaders for volunteers to fill and place sandbags. He was overwhelmed when the Church mobilized thousands of members within hours. Later, in a letter to President Spencer W. Kimball, the mayor wrote, "The faithful response of thousands of Mormons has saved Salt Lake City from major destruction and damage" (1985 *Church Almanac*, 117). Other churches and organizations also rallied to the cause.

In 1999, significant aid was sent to earthquake victims in Turkey, Greece, Taiwan and other areas. More assistance was flown to the refugees in Kosovo and flood-stricken Venezuela.

When more than a million persons were displaced by killer floods in Mozambique and Zimbabwe in 2000, the Church chartered two helicopters in South Africa to search for survivors and to begin distributing 1.3 million pounds of relief from the storehouses in Salt Lake City.

CONCLUSION

Most Latter-day Saints acknowledge, that at whatever level of performance they may be, they still have some improving to do. It has been said, when you are through changing for the better, you are through. Also, most LDS people hate to think how low, aimless and sin-filled their lives might be if it were not for the Church and its guiding principles. This does not mean that a person who is not anywhere near perfection needs to despair. A person who senses his life is improving a little has much more peace of mind than someone who is slipping. Latter-day Saints are better able to face life if they are grounded in the principles of the gospel and working together with other members to become more Christlike.

The Ostlings were at times complimentary in their book, saying, "The Mormon people encircle each other in a loving community, seeking to make sure that everyone has a divinely appointed task and that no person's needs are overlooked. In modern, fractionated American society, those are accomplishments as impressive as building a city-state on the Mississippi, hauling handcarts across the prairies, or making the arid Salt Lake Basin bloom" (Ostling and Ostling (1999), 385).

On May 13, 1999, President Gordon B. Hinckley was invited by the Los Angeles World Affairs Council to speak on the subject: "The phenomenal international influence of the Church and its increasing world-wide appeal." He capsulized what the Church was doing globally with the following personal experience which underscores Elder Marion D. Hank's answer to the London reporter at the beginning of this chapter, that the Church builds people.

"I was in Mexico City to speak to the graduating class of the school which we operate in that area. I was introduced to one of the graduates, a young woman. Her mother and her grandmother were there for the exercises. The grandmother had lived in the bush and had never learned to read or write. . . . She was baptized into the Church and had partaken of its programs, but remained illiterate. Her daughter had received a little schooling, not very much. . . . Now came this beautiful young woman. She was the third generation in the Church. She was now graduating from our school. I asked her, 'Now what are you going to do?'

"She replied, 'I have received a scholarship to the medical school at the National University.' To me that was a miracle. From the bush and total illiteracy to refinement and medical school in three generations" (www.lds.org)

The gospel of Jesus Christ gives a cure for society's existential despair and ambivalent situational ethics. It enables every person to be a winner and reach more happiness here, now and in the eternal life ahead. God does not grade on a curve. In His realms, there is room at the top for all who follow His principles as taught by The Church of Jesus Christ of Latter-day Saints.

APPENDIX A

A Few Similarities and Differences Between Today's "Mainstream Christianity" and the Church of Jesus Christ of Latter-day Saints

Nearly every semester the author has been invited to compare LDS beliefs with mainstream Christianity in a philosophy class on World Religions at the University of Utah. This is a summary of his presentation.

Mainstream Christianity	The Church of Jesus Christ of Latter-day Saints
1. Most churches stress charity and service to the needy. Christian churches often have excellent benevolent programs and Catholic Charities is an outstanding example. Christians are usually generous people.	1. The same. Supplies from Welfare storehouses are sent to disaster areas, often through the Red Cross and agencies of other churches. Service missionaries labor in needy areas. Many members donate to humanitarian causes.

2. Committed Christians attempts to live decent and righteous lives.

2. Committed Latter-day Saints strive to do the same.

3. Jesus Christ is the Savior of the world. By his agony on the cross all humans will be resurrected (See 1 Cor.15:22).

3. The same. The Book of Mormon gives further insight and witness of Jesus Christ that supplements the Bible.

4. Salvation is available to the followers of Christ. To achieve this goal, Catholics emphasize ritual (the seven sacraments). Protestants emphasize faith (enabled by the grace of Christ).

4. Similar. Latter-day Saints also emphasize works, as many Bible verses state. "Faith, if it hath not works, is dead" (James 2:17). Jesus said, "If ye love me, keep my commandments" (John 14:15).

5. Numerous Christian churches practice Christ's command to take the gospel to all the world (See Matt. 28:9; Mark 16:15).

5. The same. The LDS Church asks all worthy young men to serve two-year missions. Young women and retired married couples can also serve.

6. Christ's Second Coming will begin his Millennial reign.

6. The same. LDS do not know when this will happen.

7. Most see themselves as the true, or at least the best, church. That's why there are many different groups. All churches have similarities & differences.

7. LDS Church teaches most religions contain much truth, but post-biblical creeds have errors. Mormons claim to have the fulness of the gospel of Christ.

8. A stable marriage and family are more likely if a wife and hus-

8. The same. (Sociology studies agree: single faith homes have

band belong to the same church and participate.

9. Although doctrines differ from church to church, the moral teachings of the Bible are similar in most religions. Conservatives are more strict in their observance. Some liberal groups, for example, are lax in keeping the Sabbath day holy. Some condone abortions, homosexuality and other modern trends. Although once more common in Christianity, disciplinary action for sin is rare today.

10. Some conservative Christians consider the Bible infallible and inerrant. Liberal Christians believe it has errors. Some doubt the miracles of the Bible and question some of the sayings of Jesus.

11. Virtually all mainstream Christians espouse a closed

far less divorce, delinquency, school dropouts, etc.)

9. LDS moral teachings are similar to most other churches. Observance of God's commandments coincides more closely with conservative Christians. Members who commit serious sin are subject to Church disciplinary action. These councils of love often involve rich spiritual experiences and can help those who commit sin to repent and return to full Church fellowship.

10. Latter-day Saints have highest esteem for the Bible and its accuracy is viewed between the two mainstream positions. The Bible, as we have it today, is basically true, but has some errors, evidenced by differing versions. For example, Job says, "In my flesh shall I see God," which the Book of Mormon supports. Other translations say, *without* my flesh I shall see God:" (Job 19:26).

11. LDS have an open canon. The Bible lists lost books that canon (there is no scripture besides the Bible). To justify this view, some quote Rev. 22:18 where John says not to add to "these things." Others say this verse does not apply since Bible means "collection of books" which were added and subtracted until the Bible was finalized in A.D. 365.

12. Adam and Eve were the first of the human race and they sinned, which brought the "tragic Fall of mankind." This is why some churches teach the nature of man is evil. Some believe the Fall was a sexual sin. Some consider the Adam and Eve story a myth or figurative.

13. The Godhead is called the Trinity. Some say this means there are three gods in one. Others believe Trinity means that one God manifests himself three different ways. Some believe as Billy Graham, who said "I believe in the Trinity, but do not ask me to explain it. I can't" (*Newsweek,* May 13,1998, p. 58). The dispute

have not been found. In the Book of Mormon, Christ said that these people were among "the other sheep," he spoke of in the Bible, that he would visit (John 10:16). LDS teach revelation (scripture) still happens, since mankind today deserves and needs as much help as anciently (Amos 3:7).

12. The Fall of Adam and Eve was real, but part of God's plan to bring about a mortal experience for mankind. The conflicting commandments introduced free will. The Fall was not a result of sexual sin, since God commanded them to have children (See Gen. 1:28). Only after the Fall, becoming mortal, could Adam and Eve have children (See 2 Ne. 2: 23).

13. LDS believe in a Godhead consisting of separate beings. In over one hundred verses of the New Testament Jesus and His Father are mentioned as being separate. Paul saw Jesus on the right hand of God (See Acts 7:55). At the baptism of Jesus, the Holy Ghost was represented and the voice of the Father spoke from heaven, say-

over the Godhead is not new in our day. Before and after the Nicean council in A.D. 325, most Christians favored the view of Arius, that Jesus was a being separate and distinct from the Father. This idea was favored by church fathers Ignatius, Hermes, Justin Martyr, Origen and others. When Christianity became the official religion of the Roman Empire, bishops, who insisted on the Arian view of separateness, were replaced.

ing "This is my beloved Son" (Matt. 1:17). Several times Jesus said he did only the will of the Father who sent Him. The Trinitarian idea started at the Council of Nicea in A.D. 325 and was not fully defined until the fifth century. Latter-day Saints believe the Godhead is one in purpose, not one in personage. Mormons assert the oneness of the Godhead is only in function, not essence (See John 17:20-21).

14. Some Christians, including Unitarians and liberal factions in other churches, do not consider Christ divine, but believe he was a great moral teacher.

14. LDS testify of Christ's divinity. Additional insights in the Book of Mormon help strengthen their convictions.

15. Most Christians believe God the Father is only a spirit without body, parts, and passions.

15. The "Father has a body of flesh and bones, as tangible as man's" (D&C 130:22). God in the Bible, after the Fall, said, "The man is become as one of us" (Gen. 3:22; 1:26). Moses taught not to worship false gods who don't see, hear, eat, or smell (Deut. 4:28). Such gods would not be their true God who spoke to Moses "face to face" (Deut. 34:10). Jesus said, "he that hath seen me hath

seen the Father," meaning that since Jesus had a body, so did His Father (John 14:9).

16. Most believe Mary was a virgin when she gave birth to Jesus, based on Matt. 1:20. An angel of the Lord told her mortal husband-to-be, Joseph, "that which is conceived in [Mary] is of the Holy Ghost." Most Christians accept this verse literally. Some reject the idea of a virgin birth.

16. Mary was a virgin and LDS believe the Holy Ghost is always involved when God the Father relates to mortals. Mormons also accept the many Bible verses that speak of God being the father of Jesus. To Mary the angel said, "the Highest shall overshadow thee . . . that holy thing which shall be born of thee shall be called the Son of God" (Lk. 1:35). Other scriptures speak of Jesus as the only begotten of the Father (See John 1:14). Critics say Mormons believe God had an affair with Mary. This is *not* LDS doctrine. The method of procreation on the deity level is not known.

17. Some believe faith "alone," enabled by the grace of Christ, provides salvation. Martin Luther added the word "alone" after the word "faith." (Rom. 3:28). However other Christians believe faith "alone" is not enough.

17. Faith *and* good works are needed since the Bible mentions both. Good works and obedience to God are cited dozens of times. Romans 3:31 says faith does *not* do away with works. The Book of Mormon teaches, "It is by grace that we are saved, after all we can do" (2 Ne. 25:23).

18. Each person's existence begins with birth. Often called Ex Nihilo, meaning God created humans and the earth out of nothing.

18. God and man exist co-eternally. Before birth, we were spirit children of "the Father of spirits" (Heb. 12:9). LDS reject Ex Nihilo and accept Bible verses dealing with man's pre mortality (See Jer. 1:5; John 9:2; Eccl. 12:7; Job 38:4-7).

19. Most churches, (but not Eastern Orthodox) declare a definite, permanent distinction between God and humans. Bible scriptures that call humans the offspring of God are considered figurative. In early Christianity the deification of man concept was taught by some church leaders.

19. As with Orthodox churches, Mormons believe man is of God's species. They literally accept Christ's words, "Ye are gods; and all of you are children of the most High" (John 10:34; Ps. 82:6). God said, "Let us make man in our own image [and] likeness" (Gen.1:26).

20. God was the first cause of all creation, the first being in all existence. God was never a mere man.

20. "As man is God once was" is part of an LDS couplet that also says, "As God is man may be," spoken by Lorenzo Snow and mentioned by Joseph Smith. Although the second part of the statement is biblical, the idea of God once being a man is not. Nor is it taught in other LDS scripture. President Gordon B. Hinckley, at a 1997 press conference, said "we do not stress the idea." Mormons do not know the nature of God before "the beginning," that

251

the Bible speaks of; it is not central to LDS purposes.

21. The family is the basic, fundamental unit and strength of society. All churches seem to be giving it more attention since it is apparent that many families today are in serious jeopardy.

21. The same. Latter-day Saints believe the doctrine of eternal families is a powerful incentive to commit families to Christ, and helps in raising decent children. For those who die without the blessing of being sealed as eternal families, LDS members perform the rites by proxy in LDS temples.

22. Considered a monotheistic religion, but Moslems claim they are the only real monotheistic religion.

22. Critics wrongly call LDS polytheists. The dictionary says polytheists worship many gods, but LDS do not. Other gods, however, do exist. Six Bible verses speak of "God of gods" (Deut.10:17). Paul spoke of many gods (1 Cor. 8:5).

23. Anthropomorphism is the idea that man creates a god in man's image. Most Christians reject this idea, believing God is without body, parts or passions as post-biblical creeds declared.

23. Latter-day Saints are accused of being anthropomorphic, but technically are not. Believing that God created man in God's image is different from man creating God in man's image (Gen. 1:26; 3:22).

24. Biblical references to Satan and Hell (a place of fire and brimstone) are considered figurative by many. However, some

24. Latter-day Saints believe in a literal Satan (devil). They do not believe hell is a place of eternal burning. Such verses are

Christians accept the verses about Satan and Hell literally.

only descriptive of suffering that unrepentant sinners will undergo (2 Ne. 9:16; D&C 19:10).

25. A hierarchy governs Catholic and Eastern Orthodox churches. Protestant churches have various forms of parliamentary type leadership structures.

25. The LDS Church is a hierarchy headed by apostles and prophets, etc. Eph. 4:11-13 states that these offices should exist "until we all come in the unity of the faith."

26. Catholic and Eastern Orthodox churches claim direct priesthood authority that they can trace to the chief apostle Peter. Protestants believe in a "priesthood of all believers," rejecting the idea that direct authority from God is necessary for church leadership.

26. God's priesthood authority was lost following death of apostles as Paul prophesied (See 2 Thes. 2:3). John the Baptist came and restored the Aaronic Priesthood to Joseph Smith and Oliver Cowdery. Peter, James and John, Christ's three main apostles, restored the Melchizedek Priesthood.

27. Christian churches believe in a heaven. Catholics also have limbo and purgatory concepts.

27. At death our spirits go to paradise or spirit prison (See Lk. 23: 43; 1 Pet. 4:6). The resurrection and Christ's judgement follow to determine one of the three kingdoms of glory or outer darkness, where we will dwell (See 2 Cor. 12:2; 1 Cor. 15:40; John 14:2).

28. Salvation is a personal quest that involves coming to

28. Similar. LDS believe Christ's love for us is so great

Jesus Christ, and accepting His love.

that He wants us to become like God. This includes continuation of family if parents are wed in the House of the Lord (an LDS temple) and continue to keep their marriage vows.

29. The eternal goal is to go to be with God.

29. The eternal goal is to be like God and continue in his service, and be "encircled eternally in the arms of His love" (2 Ne. 1:15).

BIBLIOGRAPHY

<u>Books Cited</u>

Allen, Joseph L. *Exploring the Lands of the Book of Mormon.* 1989.

Anderson, Richard Lloyd, *Investigating the Book of Mormon Witnesses.* 1980.

Andrus, Hyrum, *Joseph Smith and World Government.* 1958.

Answers For Young Latter-day Saints. (Numerous authors). 1998.

Arrington, Leonard J., *Brigham Young: American Moses.* 1985.

_____. *Great Basin Kingdom: An Economic History of the Latter-day Saints.* 1958.

_____ and Bitton, David, *The Mormon Experience.* 1979.

Aston, Warren P. and Michaela K., *In the Footsteps of Lehi: New Evidence for Lehi's Journey Across Arabia to Bountiful.* 1994.

Ayres, Alex, ed., *The Wit and Wisdom of Mark Twain.* 1987.

Backman, Milton V. Jr., *American Religions and the Rise of Mormonism.* 1965.

_____. *Joseph Smith's First Vision.* 1980.

Blomberg, Craig L. and Stephen E. Robinson, *How Wide the Divide? A Mormon & Evangelical in Conversation.* 1997.

Brauch, Manfred T., *Hard Sayings of Paul.* 1989.

Brewster, Hoyt W., *Isaiah Plain and Simple.* 1995.

Brooks, Juanita, *The Mountain Meadows Massacre.* Rev. ed. 1985.

Brown, Robert L. and Rosemary, *They Lie In Wait to*

Deceive. 4 vols. 1992–1994.

Bruce, F. F., *Hard Sayings of Jesus.* 1983.

Bushman, Richard L., *Joseph Smith and the Beginnings of Mormonism.* 1985.

_____. *Ancient Writing on Metal Plates.* 1985.

Clark, James R., ed., *Messages of the First Presidency.* 5 vol. 1965.

Cross, Whitney R., *The Burned Over District.* 1950.

Crowther, Duane S., *The Prophecies of Joseph Smith.* 1997.

Decker, Ed and Dave Hunt, *The Godmakers.* 1984.

Duke, James T., *Latter-day Saints Social Life.* 1998.

Durham, Reed C. Jr. and Steven H. Heath, *Succession in the Church.* 1970.

Gentry, Leland, "History of the Latter-day Saints in Northern Missouri." Ph.D. dissertation, Brigham Young University, 1965.

Gibbons, Francis M., *Joseph Smith: Martyr, Prophet of God.* 1997.

Gibson, Stephen R., *One Minute Answers to Anti-Mormon Questions.* 1995.

Godfrey, Kenneth W., "Causes of Mormon/Non-Mormon Conflict in Hancock County." Ph.D. dissertation, Brigham Young University, 1967.

Gorton, H. Clay, *The Legacy of the Brass Plates of Laban.* 1994.

Griffith, Michael T., *A Ready Reply: Answering Challenging Questions About the Gospel.* 1994.

————————. *Refuting the Critics.* 1993.

————————. *Signs of the True Church of Christ.* 1989.

Hansen, Klaus J., *Quest for Empire.* 1967.

Hartley, William G., *They Were My Friends.* 1986.

Heaton, Tim B., Thomas Hirschl, and Bruce A. Chadwick, *Utah in the 1990s.* 1996.

Hickenbotham, Michael W., *Answering Challenging Mormon Questions.* 1995.

Hill, Donna, *Joseph Smith, The First Mormon.* 1977.

Hopkins, Richards R., *Biblical Mormonism: Responding to Evangelical Criticism of LDS Theology.* 1995.

Jesse, Dean C., ed., *The Personal Writings of Joseph Smith.* 1984.

Kaiser, Walter C. Jr., *Hard Sayings of the Old Testament.* 1988.

Larson, Gustive O., *Outline History of Utah and the Mormons.* 1958.

Lewis, C. S., *The Weight and the Glory and Other Addresses,* Rev. ed. 1990.

Ludlow, Daniel H., ed., *Encyclopedia of Mormonism.* 5 vols. 1992.

_____. *A Companion to Your Study of*

the Book of Mormon. 1976

_____. *A Companion to Your Study of the Doctrine and Covenants*. 1978.

Ludlow, Victor L., *Principles and Practices of the Restored Gospel*. 1992.

Martin, Thomas K; Tim B. Heaton and Stephen J. Bahr, *Utah in Demographic Perspective*. 1986.

Matthews, Robert J., *Who's Who in the Book of Mormon*. 1966.

McConkie, Bruce R., *Mormon Doctrine*, 2nd ed., 1966.

McConkie, Joseph Fielding and Robert Millet, *Sustaining and Defending the Faith*. Salt Lake City: 1980.

_____. *Answers*. 1998.

Mulder, William, ed., *Among the Mormons*. 1973.

Nibley, Hugh W., *An Approach to the Book of Mormon*. 1964.

_____. *Since Cumorah.* 1967.

Nyman, Monte S., *Great Are the Words of Isaiah.* 1980.

Oaks, Dallin H. and Marvin S. Hill, *Carthage Conspiracy: The Trial of the Accused Assassins of Joseph Smith.* 1979.

O'Dea, Thomas F., *The Mormons.* 1957.

Odegard, Peter H., *Religion and Politics.* 1960.

Ostling, Richard H. and Joan K., *Mormon America.* 1999.

Padover, Saul K., *The Meaning of Democracy.* 1963.

Palmer, Spencer J., *The Expanding Church.* 1978.

Peterson, Daniel C. and Stephen D. Ricks, *Offenders For a Word–How Anti-Mormons Play Word Games to Attack the Latter-day Saints.* 1992.

Phipps, William E., *Was Jesus Married?* 1970.

Quinn, D. Michael, *Mormonism and Magic.* 1987.

Quincey, Josiah, *Figures of the Past.* 1896.

Reynolds, Noel B., ed., *Book of Mormon Authorship: New Light on Ancient Origins.* 1982.

_____. ed., *Book of Mormon Authorship Revisited: The Evidence for Ancient Origins.* 1997.

Ricks, Stephen D. and John W. Welch, eds., *The Allegory of the Olive Tree.* 1994.

Roberts, B. H, *A Comprehensive History of the Church of Jesus Christ of Latter-day Saints.* 6 vols. 1930.

Robinson, Stephen E., *Are Mormons Christians?* 1991.

Rudd, Glen L., *Pure Religion.* 1995.

Rust, Richard Dilworth, *Feasting on the Word: The Literary Testimony of the Book of Mormon.* 1997.

Scharffs, Gilbert W., *Mormonism in Germany.* 1970.

_____. *The Truth About the Godmakers.* 2nd ed., 1989.

_____. *101 Reasons Why I Like to Go to Church:* 1983.

Sillitoe, Linda and Allen Roberts, *Salamander, The Story of the Mormon Forgery Murders.* 1988.

Smith, Joseph, *History of the Church of Jesus Christ of Latter-day Saints.* 7 vols. 1902–1912.

Smith, Joseph Fielding, *Answers to Gospel Questions* 5 vols. 1957–1966.

_____. *Essential in Church History.* 18th ed. 1963.

_____. comp., *Teachings of the Prophet Joseph Smith.* 1938.

Sorenson, John L., *An Ancient American Setting for the Book of Mormon.* 1985.

_____. *Metals and Metallurgy Relating to the Book of Mormon Text.* 1992.

_____. and Raish, Martin H., eds.,
*Pre-Columbian Contact with America Across
the Oceans: An Annotated Bibliography.* 2
vols. 1990.

_____. and Thorne, Melvin J., eds..,
Rediscovering the Book of Mormon. 1991.

Stevens, John Lloyd, *Incidents of Travel in Central
America, Chiapas, and Yucatan.* 2 vols.
1969. (First published in 1841.)

Stromberg, Roland W., *Religious Liberalsim.* 1954.

Sweet, William Warren, *Religion in the Development
of American Culture.* 1952.

Talmage, James E., *The Story and Philosophy of
Mormonism.* 1930.

Turley, Richard E. Jr., *Victims: The LDS Church and
the Mark Hofmann Case.* 1992.

Van Doren, *Benjamin Franklin.* 1938.

Vetterli, Richard, *Mormonism, Americanism and
American Politics.* 1961.

Welch, John W., ed., *Reexploring the Book of Mormon.* 1992.

_____. *The Sermon at the Temple and the Sermon on the Mount.* 1990.

Winwood, Richard I., *Take Heed That Ye Be Not Deceived.* 1995.

Articles Cited

Allen, James B., "Eight Contemporary Accounts of Joseph Smith's First Vision." *Improvement Era,* Apr. 1970, 4–13.

_____. "The Significance of Joseph Smith's 'First Vision' in Mormon Thought. *Dialogue,* vol. 4 (Autumn 1966), 28–45.

Anderson, Richard L., "I Have a Question," *Ensign,* Apr. 1987, 23–27.

Asay, Carlos E., "Opposition to the Work of God," *Ensign,* Nov. 1981, 67–68.

Benson, Ezra Taft, *Deseret News,* 16 September 1976, 23.

Bushman, Richard L., "The First Vision Revisited,"
        Dialogue, vol. 4 (Spring 1969), 82–93.

Crowell, Angela, "Hebraisms in the Book of
        Mormon," *Zarahemla Record,* Summer and
        Fall, 1982, 1–7, 16.

England, Eugene, *Through the Arabian Desert to a
        Bountiful Land.* Reprint. 1996.

Esplin, Ronald K., "Joseph, Brigham and the
        Twelve: A Succession of Continuity," *BYU
        Studies,* Summer 1981, 319–320.

Hale, Van, *How Could a Prophet Believe in Moonmen*
        [pamphlet]. 1982.

_____. *What About the Adam God
        Theory,* [pamphlet]. 1982.

Huntington, Oliver B., *Young Women's Journal,*
        1892, 3:263.

Jakeman, M. Wells, "Stela Five, Izapa, Chiapas,
        Mexico," *University Archaeological
        Newsletter,* 1958.

Jessee, Dean C., "The Early Accounts of Joseph Smith's First Vision." *BYU Studies,* vol. 9 (Spring 1969), 275–294.

Kimball, Stanley B., "Kinderhook Plates Brought to Joseph Smith Appear to be a Nineteenth Century Hoax." *Ensign,* Aug. 1981, 66–74.

McConkie, Bruce R., "The Caravan Moves On," *Ensign,* Nov. 1984, 82–85.

Murphy, Thomas W., "Re-inventing Mormonism," *Sunstone,* 29:172–192: 1996.

Nelson, Russell M., "Truth—and More," *Ensign,* Feb. 1987, 69–73.

Oaks, Dallin H., "Criticism," *Ensign,* Feb. 1987, 68–69.

Quinn, D. Michael, "The Council of Fifty and its Members, 1844-1845. *BYU Studies* (Winter 1945, 52–53.

Reynolds, Noel B., "Shedding New Light on Ancient Origins," *Brigham Young Magazine,* Spring 1998, 36–45.

Scharffs, Gilbert W., "I Have a Question," *Ensign,* Jan. 1985, 52–53.

Stark, Rodney, "Extracting Social Scientific Models from Mormon History," *Journal of Mormon History,* vol. 24, no. 1 (Spring 1999), 174.

Stewart, D. Michael, *"I Have a Question," Ensign,* June 1976, 64–65.

Tvedtness, John, "I Have a Question," *Ensign,* October 1986, 64–66.

Works Not Formally Published

Cheesman, Paul R., "An Analysis of the Accounts Relating to Joseph Smith's Early Visions." master's thesis, Brigham Young University, 1965.

ABOUT THE AUTHOR

Gilbert W. Scharffs received a bachelor of arts degree in marketing from the University of Utah, a master's degree in business from New York University, and his Ph.D. in history of religion and Bible and modern scripture from BYU.

He has taught religion classes in the education system of The Church of Jesus Christ of Latter-day Saints in seminary, at BYU, and for 27 years at the LDS Institute of Religion adjacent to the University of Utah, where he also served as the director for a number of years.

He is the author of *Mormonism in Germany, 101 Reasons Why I Like to Go to Church, The Truth About the Godmakers*, and several articles for Church magazines. He also publishes the Utah Symphony program magazine for each concert.

He and his first wife, Virginia (now deceased) are the parents of Yvette, Brett, Lisa, and Calvin.

Brother Scharffs recently married Judy Short, who has taught and coached in the Granite and Jordan school districts.